£2.95

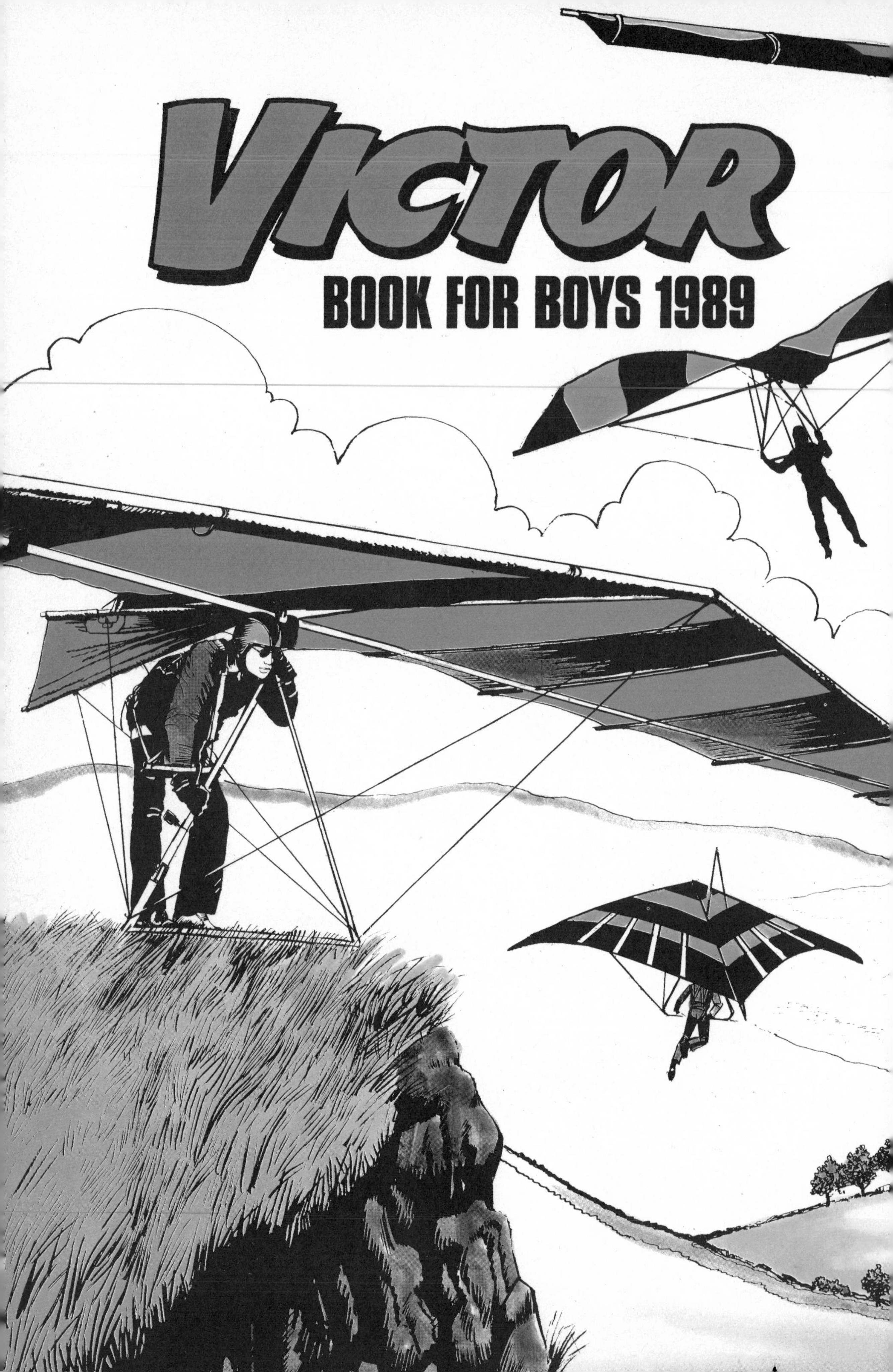
VICTOR
BOOK FOR BOYS 1989

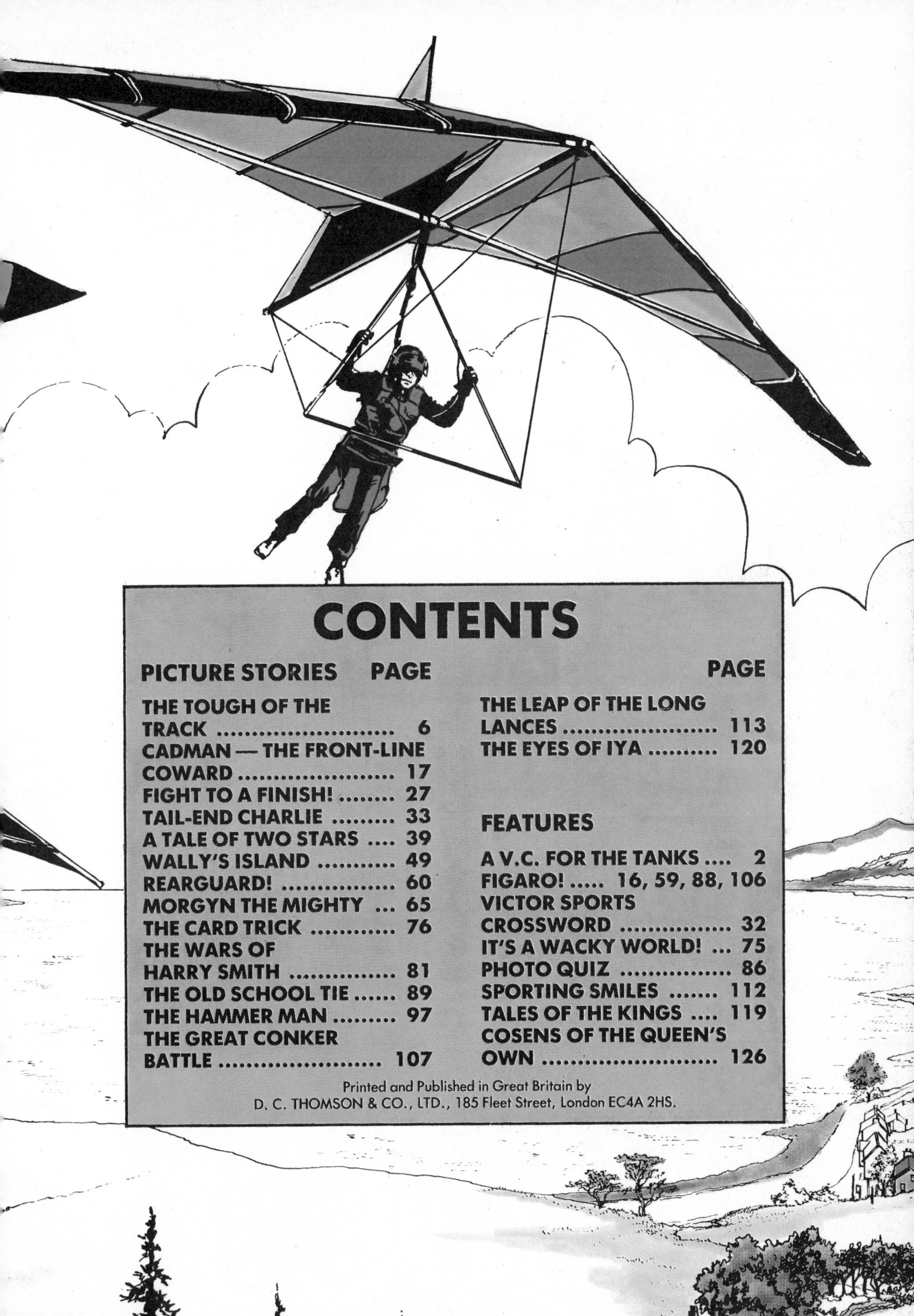

CONTENTS

Printed and Published in Great Britain by
D. C. THOMSON & CO., LTD., 185 Fleet Street, London EC4A 2HS.

THE TOUGH OF THE TRACK
Alf Tupper, the runner known as the Tough of the Track, was out on a training run through the streets of Greystone, the industrial town where he lived.
HI THERE, ALF. IN TRAINING FOR THE MILLERTON MILE NEXT SATURDAY, EH?
YOU BET, DICK. I'M GOING TO RUN 'EM!
The Millerton Mile was an annual event at the Greystone sports centre. Alf had won the last two and was keen to make it three in a row.
JUST TIME TO GET MY FISH 'N' CHIPS BEFORE THEY CLOSE.
P.C. CROSS WAS IN HERE EARLIER ASKING IF I'D SEEN YOU, ALF.
TOM? PROBABLY ABOUT THE GREYSTONE MARATHON NEXT MONTH. I ASKED HIM TO GET ME AN ENTRY FORM.
Alf lived under the railway arches where he had a one-man welding business.
ALF TUPPER
DONE HERE
HI, TOM — YOU'RE JUST IN TIME FOR A CHIP. DID YOU GET THOSE ENTRY FORMS?
NO, NOT YET, ALF. I'M AFRAID THIS VISIT IS OFFICIAL.

THERE HAVE BEEN SEVERAL BURGLARIES IN THE AREA RECENTLY, ALF. BILL FERNLY'S PLACE WAS DONE OVER LAST NIGHT WHILE HE WAS DOWN AT THE LOCAL.

BILL SPOTTED A RUNNER WITH A WOLF'S HEAD BADGE ON HIS SINGLET COMING OUT OF THE ALLEY AT THE BACK OF HIS HOUSE LAST NIGHT. TWO OTHER BURGLARY VICTIMS REPORT SEEING THE SAME RUNNER.
ME?

OH, COME ON NOW, TOM! YOU DON'T REALLY BELIEVE I —
OF COURSE NOT, ALF — BUT YOU WEAR A SINGLET WITH A WOLF'S HEAD BADGE, SO I'VE GOT TO GO THROUGH THE MOTIONS.

ALL RIGHT, OFFICER, I'LL COME CLEAN. I WAS NOWHERE NEAR BILL FERNLY'S PLACE LAST NIGHT. I DID MY TRAINING OVER PARKTON WAY.
I'M GOING TO HAVE TO SEARCH YOUR PLACE, ALF.

THIS IS CRAZY, TOM! YOU KNOW I'M NO SNEAK THIEF!
OF COURSE I DO, ALF. THIS IS JUST ROUTINE. CALM DOWN.

P.C. Cross found nothing.
THANKS, ALF. NOW I CAN GO BACK TO THE STATION AND PUT INSPECTOR FAWCETTE'S MIND AT REST.
TUPPER
DONE HERE
PROPER THING, TOO. DON'T FORGET THOSE MARATHON ENTRY FORMS, TOM.

Alf was out training again that evening.
HELLO, LOOKS LIKE THERE'S BEEN AN ACCIDENT.

THAT'S HIM! EEEEK! HE'S THE ONE!
JUST A MOMENT, SIR!
LOOK, I'VE BEEN THROUGH ALL THIS ONCE TODAY! I TELL YOU I'M NO SNEAK THIEF!
YOU CAN MAKE A FULL STATEMENT DOWN AT THE STATION, SIR.
At the police station —
IT'S HIM, I TELL YOU! SAW HIM PLAIN AS DAY! I'D JUST GOT BACK FROM BINGO AND HE CAME DASHING OUT OF MY HOUSE AND KNOCKED ME DOWN! TAKEN ALL MY SAVINGS, HE HAD.
I DID NO SUCH THING, MRS COLVER! IT WASN'T ME!
I JUST HEARD THE NEWS, ALF.
TOM, THANK HEAVENS YOU'RE HERE! TELL 'EM, WILL YOU? THERE'S BEEN A MISTAKE!
NOW THINK CAREFULLY, MRS COLVER. DID YOU ACTUALLY SEE THIS YOUNG MAN'S FACE AS HE CAME OUT OF YOUR HOME?
WELL, I DIDN'T SEE HIS FACE VERY WELL, 'COS HE TOOK ME BY SURPRISE — BUT I SAW THAT HORRIBLE LOOKING ANIMAL ON HIS VEST! HE WANTS LOCKING UP!
YES, MRS COLVER. WELL, THAT WILL BE ALL FOR NOW. WE'LL KEEP IN TOUCH.
Alf was free to leave.
I'VE NOT BEEN ARRESTED, BUT I'M STILL THE NUMBER ONE SUSPECT, AREN'T I, TOM?
OBVIOUSLY THE THIEF IS TRYING TO THROW SUSPICION ON YOU AND DIVERT IT FROM HIMSELF, ALF. HE MUST HAVE SEEN YOU IN YOUR SINGLET LOTS OF TIMES.
The following evening —
IT IS MISTY AND RAINING. NOT A VERY NICE EVENING FOR TRAINING, BUT I INTEND BUSTING THE TRACK RECORD ON SATURDAY. THAT'S IF I'M NOT LOCKED UP!

Suddenly through the mist, Alf spotted another runner.
BLOOMING ADA! THAT RUNNER'S GOT A WOLF'S HEAD BADGE — AND HE'S COMING OUT OF PHIL GARVIN'S PLACE!
Alf gave chase.
HE CAN CERTAINLY MOVE! GREAT LOPING STRIDES!
But the mist thickened.
BLAST! WHICH WAY DID HE GO?
Alf gave up the chase and returned to Phil Garvin's home.
YOU'RE RIGHT, ALF — SOMEBODY'S BEEN TRYING TO FORCE MY WINDOW!
HE MUST HAVE HEARD ME COMING AND TOOK OFF, PHIL.
Alf reported the incident to the police.
HE WAS WEARING A SINGLET LIKE YOURS AND CARRYING A HIKER'S DAY-SACK, BUT YOU DIDN'T SEE HIS FACE AND YOU LOST HIM IN THE MIST. PITY ABOUT THAT, EH, LAD?
YOU THINK I'M MAKING THIS UP, DON'T YOU, SERGEANT? YOU STILL THINK I'M THE THIEF!
Alf was still angry on Saturday.
MILLEATON MILE.
OPEN TO ALLCOMERS
HI, TOM. HAVE YOUR SUPER-SLEUTHS SEEN ANY MORE OF MY PHANTOM LOOK-ALIKE?
GREYSTONE SPORTS CENTRE
DRESSING ROOM
OUCH! GO EASY, ALF. I'M ON YOUR SIDE, REMEMBER.

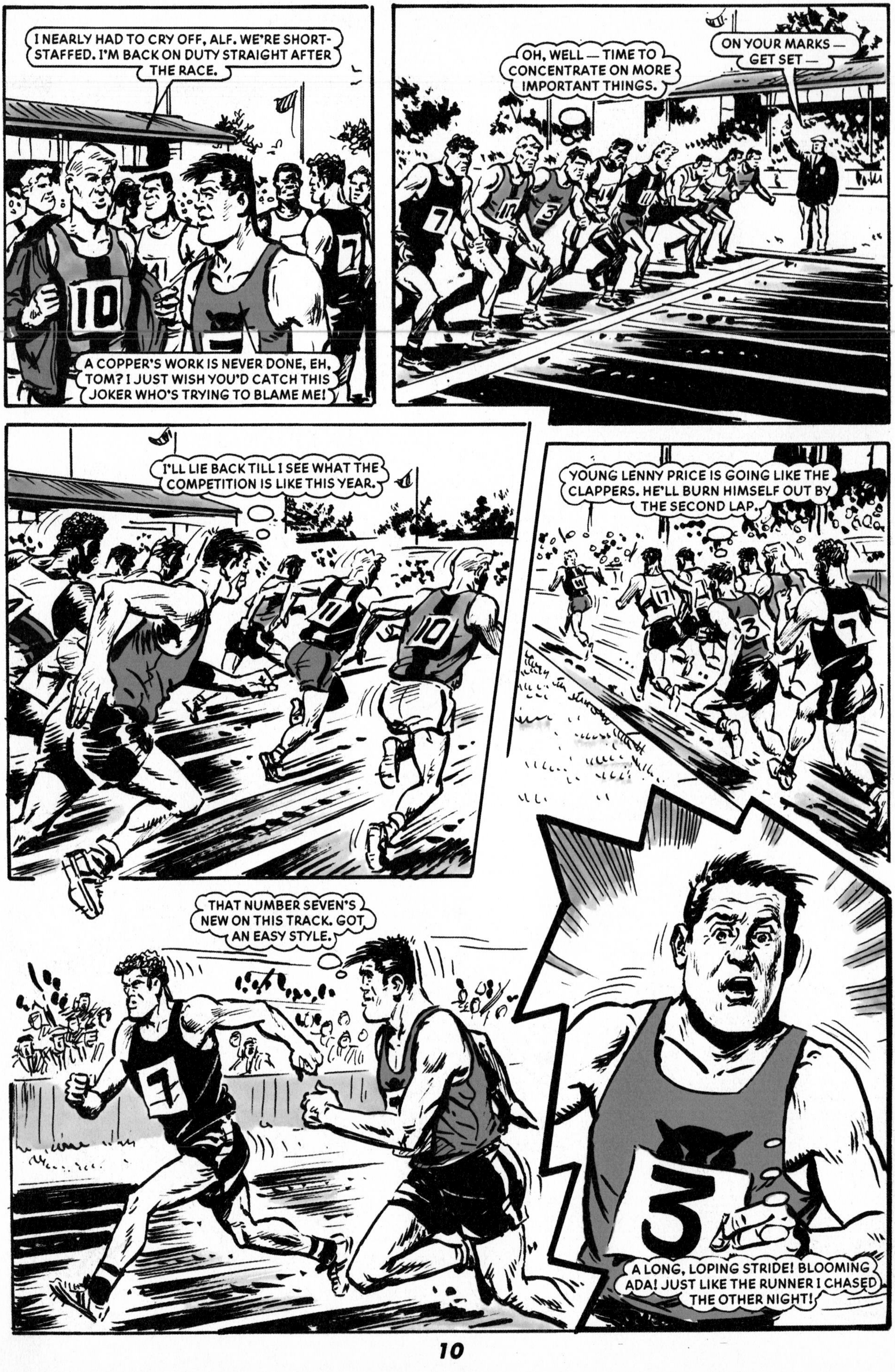

I'LL LIE BACK TILL I SEE WHAT THE COMPETITION IS LIKE THIS YEAR.

YOUNG LENNY PRICE IS GOING LIKE THE CLAPPERS. HE'LL BURN HIMSELF OUT BY THE SECOND LAP.

THAT NUMBER SEVEN'S NEW ON THIS TRACK. GOT AN EASY STYLE.

A LONG, LOPING STRIDE! BLOOMING ADA! JUST LIKE THE RUNNER I CHASED THE OTHER NIGHT!

IT'S HIM! I'M SURE OF IT!
Alf was in third place at the bell.
IF ONLY I'D BEEN ABLE TO GET A LOOK AT HIS FACE.
Alf pushed all other thoughts from his mind. There was a race to be won.
HE'S READY TO BREAK!
RIGHT ABOUT NOW!
GO IT, ALF! HE'S THERE!
YOU MADE ME WORK FOR THAT, MATE. DON'T THINK WE'VE MET.
SPEED — FRANK SPEED. YOU RUN A GOOD RACE.

IF THAT IS OUR THIEF, HE'S CERTAINLY A COOL CUSTOMER!
WELL DONE, ALF. YOU LOST ME, MATE.
SEE THAT NUMBER SEVEN, TOM? FRANK SPEED. THAT'S HIM — THE SNEAK THIEF — I'M SURE OF IT! I RECOGNISE THE RUNNING STYLE. IT'S A DEAD GIVE-AWAY!
Alf changed quickly, and was outside when Speed emerged from the dressing-room.
WHERE IS HE, ALF?
CAR PARK
JUST GOING INTO THE CAR PARK.
Tom and Alf followed Frank Speed to the outskirts of Greystone.
HE'S TURNING IN, TOM. THAT MUST BE HIS HOUSE.
WE'LL PAY MR SPEED A SURPRISE VISIT, ALF.
MR FRANK SPEED? I'M CONSTABLE TOM CROSS. CAN I HAVE A FEW WORDS WITH YOU, SIR?
WHAT ABOUT?
ABOUT A SINGLET WITH A WOLF'S HEAD BADGE ON IT, MATE — AND QUITE A FEW BURGLARIES!
WELL, WELL — WHAT HAVE WE HERE? A PROPER LITTLE ALADDIN'S CAVE!
YOU'VE NO RIGHT TO GO IN THERE!
NO, JUST A MOMENT, SIR!
Speed turned nasty.
WATCH IT, TOM!
AAAARGH!

Alf moved quickly.
YOU AIN'T GOING NOWHERE, MATE!
AAAARGH!
TWO, FIVE, TWO TO CONTROL!
A few minutes later —
ARE YOU OKAY, TOM?
I'M FINE, ALF. THANKS FOR YOUR HELP.
I'LL GET YOU FOR THIS — BOTH OF YOU!
The following month —
WELL, FRANK SPEED GOT WHAT HE DESERVED.
SNEAK THIEF SENTENCED TO THREE YEARS
OW! MY FOOT!
THAT'LL TEACH ME TO LOOK WHERE I'M GOING. BLOOMING ADA — AND IT'S THE GREYSTONE PEOPLE'S MARATHON ON SATURDAY!
Saturday —
HOW'S THE FOOT, ALF?
STILL PAINFUL, TOM. I DON'T RECKON I'LL BE BREAKING ANY RECORDS TODAY.

I DON'T WANT TO WORRY YOU, ALF, BUT SPEED DID A RUNNER FROM CUSTODY LAST NIGHT. BEST KEEP YOUR EYES OPEN. HE'S A BIT OF A NUTTER.
BLOOMING ADA! HE THREATENED TO GET EVEN WITH US, TOM!

MORE THAN LIKELY HE'LL GET AS FAR AWAY FROM THIS AREA AS POSSIBLE.
SO LONG AS HE DOESN'T GET UP TO HIS OLD TRICKS AND PRETEND TO BE ME!
ON YOUR MARKS — GET SET —

I'M HOPING TO BEAT MY LAST YEAR'S TIME, ALF. I WAS FORTY-FIFTH.
THEN IT'S NO USE YOU TAGGING ALONG WITH ME, MATE. WITH MY GAMMY FOOT I'LL DO WELL TO FINISH AT ALL.

As the field began to string out —
I'LL PRESS ON THEN, ALF. TOO BAD ABOUT YOUR FOOT.
SERVES ME RIGHT. YOU RUN 'EM FOR ME, TOM. GOOD LUCK, MATE!

BLOOMIN' ADA! THE CAVEMAN! IT'S FRANK SPEED! IF HE GETS TOM ON HIS OWN —

Alf forced himself on painfully —
TOM!

— and went in, fists flying.
THAT UGLY MUG DON'T FOOL ME, SPEED!
AAAARGH!
Other runners summoned help, and minutes later —
ARE YOU ALL RIGHT, TOM?
JUST ABOUT, ALF — THANKS TO YOU. I'D BEST GO BACK TO THE STATION.
POLICE
Later —
YES, THERE WAS QUITE A SCUFFLE, THEY SAY. SPEED SET ABOUT TOM CROSS WITH A CLUB.
HERE COME MORE OF THE FUN RUNNERS. WHO'S THE JOKER IN THE CAVEMAN MASK?
HI, FELLERS. I FINALLY MADE IT!
IT'S ALF! WHAT ARE YOU DOING WITH THE MASK, MATE?
IT'S LIKE THIS, LADS — WITH A TIME LIKE THAT, I HARDLY DARED SHOW MY FACE!
The End

FIGARO

WATCH ME ROB THIS BANK, FIGARO FANS!
SHERIFF'S OFFICE
BANK

STOP, THIEF!
SUCCESS!
BANK

QUICK, SHERIFF! AFTER THAT ROBBER!

THIS SHERIFF'S A FAST RUNNER!...

TOO FAST FOR ME!
BANK

HEIGH-HO! JAILED AGAIN!
OH-OH! MY OIL CAN'S LEAKING!

HO! HO! SLIPPERY STUFF, OIL!

NOW THERE'S A WAY TO STOP THAT SPEEDY SHERIFF!

SIX DAYS LATER...
RIGHT, FIGARO! YOU'VE SERVED YOUR SENTENCE!
I'LL GO STRAIGHT TO THE GENERAL STORE!

A GALLON OF OIL, PLEASE!
RIGHT, SIR!
OIL

NOW I CAN ROB THE BANK IN SAFETY!
SHERIFF'S OFFICE

...IF THE SHERIFF RUNS OUT AFTER ME, HE'LL JUST SLIP ABOUT ON THE OIL!
BANK

HELP! SHERIFF!
BANK

ULP! THE SHERIFF!
FIGARO!

HAVE TO ESCAPE THIS WAY!
STOP!

OOPS! I FORGOT ABOUT THE OIL!
BANK

HUH! I SHOULD HAVE MADE SURE HE WAS INSIDE HIS OFFICE BEFORE I PUT DOWN THAT OIL!

CADMAN THE FRONT-LINE COWARD

Captain Gerald Cadman, V.C., better known by Corporal Tom Smith as a cowardly rogue, found himself at the wrong end of a German bayonet charge during confused fighting on the Flanders battlefront in 1917.

AAH!

VORWARTS! CHARGE!

THE JERRIES HAVE GOT OUR HERO ON THE HOP AGAIN!

TAKE COVER IN THIS BUSTED TANK, SIR!

GAD! HOW DID WE GET SO FAR AHEAD OF OUR OWN TROOPS, SMITH?
SEARCH ME! HE'S USUALLY WELL BACK AT THE REAR!

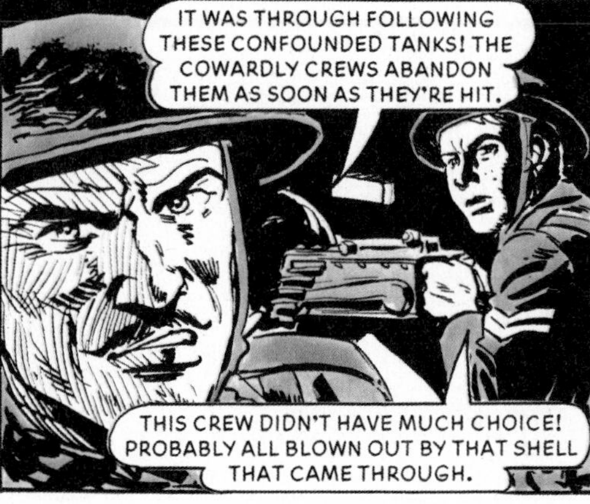

IT WAS THROUGH FOLLOWING THESE CONFOUNDED TANKS! THE COWARDLY CREWS ABANDON THEM AS SOON AS THEY'RE HIT.
THIS CREW DIDN'T HAVE MUCH CHOICE! PROBABLY ALL BLOWN OUT BY THAT SHELL THAT CAME THROUGH.

THE DEUCED HUNS ARE STILL COUNTER-ATTACKING!
THAT'S STOPPED SOME OF 'EM!

YOU TAKE OVER AT THE VICKERS NOW, SIR, WHILE I SEE IF THIS TIN-CAN MIGHT STILL GO ENOUGH TO GET US BACK.

Some minutes later, at a British front-line trench —
BOMB THE TOMMIES OUT!
ACHTUNG! BEHIND US!

HIMMEL! TOMMIES IN FRONT! TANK AT REAR! WE'RE TRAPPED!

Soon, at battalion HQ —
SPLENDID WORK, CAPTAIN! YOUR STUNT WITH THAT TANK CAPTURED A FAIR NUMBER OF ENEMY ASSAULT TROOPS!
JUST AS I INTENDED, OF COURSE, COLONEL!

YOU DESERVE THIS LITTLE REST-CURE OF A JOB BEHIND THE LINES!
SPOT OF WORK AT STAFF HQ?

NOT EXACTLY! TEMPORARY COMMAND OF A PRISONER-OF-WAR TRANSIT CAMP.
OH, WELL! IT GETS ME OUT OF THE FIRING-LINE FOR A WHILE!

Next day —
JERRY PRISONERS GET PUT HERE WHILE WAITING FOR A TRANSFER TO ENGLAND AND OTHER PLACES, EH, SIR?

SO HOW LONG DO WE GET STUCK HERE?
COMMANDANT
UNTIL A MORE REGULAR COMMANDANT IS APPOINTED. THIS CAMP IS ONLY A TEMPORARY SET-UP DUE TO LARGE NUMBERS OF ENEMY CAPTURED RECENTLY.

VERY SLACK, SERGEANT! WHY WAS NO GUARD PARADED FOR YOUR NEW COMMANDING OFFICER?
A CHANCE TO THROW HIS WEIGHT ABOUT IN SAFETY!

HARD-LOOKING LOT O' JERRIES!
ALL HUNS RESPECT PROPER AUTHORITY!

HAUPTMANN KRANZ! SENIOR GERMAN OFFICER! AT YOUR ORDERS, HERR CAPTAIN!
DISMISS YOUR MEN, HAUPTMANN!

I'M NOT TOO HAPPY ABOUT THINGS HERE, CAPTAIN.
NEITHER AM I, LIEUTENANT BATES! THE HUNS ARE FAR SMARTER THAN YOUR GUARD SQUAD!

I KNOW, BUT THERE'S SOMETHING ELSE —
DON'T ARGUE! THERE WILL BE EXTRA DRILL PARADES FOR ALL THE CAMP GUARDS! I'LL SHOW YOU HOW TO SMARTEN THEM UP!

OUR BLOKES HERE AREN'T UP TO THIS SORT OF DRILL, CORP. MOSTLY UNFIT FOR THE FRONT. THEY CAN'T SPARE FIGHTING TROOPS FOR CAMPS LIKE THIS.
DOUBLE MARCH! KEEP THOSE RIFLES UP!

SO WHAT'S WORRYING YOUR OFFICER, SARGE?
ENEMY PLANES FLEW OVER THE OTHER DAY AND HE THINKS THEY DROPPED ESCAPE MESSAGES TO THE PRISONERS.

WHAT ABOUT THIS TALK OF THE JERRIES PLANNING A BREAK-OUT, SIR? AFTER ALL, WE'RE NOT FAR BEHIND OUR LINES HERE.
CAMP COMMANDANT
PIFFLE! NOW I'M TIRED AFTER THOSE DRILL PARADES. IT'S NOT AN OFFICER'S JOB. YOU TAKE OVER TOMORROW.

That night at a guard hut —
BLIMEY, THEY'RE ALL KIPPING! WAKEY-WAKEY, LADS!

SORRY, CORP! WE'RE DONE IN AFTER ALL THAT DRILL.
NO EXCUSE, CHUM! GET YOUR SENTRIES OUT!

Later —
ENEMY GUN BARRAGE. THE HUNS HAVE LAUNCHED A BIG ATTACK. I'M GLAD WE'RE NOT UP THERE AT THE FRONT NOW!

Suddenly —
GAD! A HUN AIR ATTACK!

URGH! THEY'RE DROPPING BOMBS! TAKE COVER!
THE JERRIES WOULDN'T BOMB A POW CAMP.

STREUTH! JERRY RIFLES AND GRENADES!

AAH!
HANDS OFF, TOMMY!

QUICK, SIR! SOUND AN ALARM! THOSE PLANES DROPPED WEAPONS!
SO I SEE! KEEP DOWN OR THEY'LL KILL US!

TURN OUT THE GUARD!
HOW DARE YOU TAKE MY PISTOL!

TOO BLINKING LATE! TAKE IT BACK!
HANDE HOCH! HANDS UP, TOMMIES!

URGH! DON'T SHOOT!
NO NEED, HERR CAPTAIN! MY MEN ALREADY SURROUND YOUR MAIN GUARD HUT. YOU AND ONE CORPORAL CANNOT STOP US NOW.

OUR ESCAPE WAS WELL PLANNED. WE CAN NOW ATTACK YOUR FRONT LINES FROM THE REAR EXACTLY WHERE OUR MAIN OFFENSIVE IS PLANNED TO BREAK THROUGH.

Back at the camp office —
JUST RIP OUT THE TELEPHONE AND TAKE ANY PAPERS OF VALUE FROM THE DESK, SCHNELL! QUICKLY NOW!
BANG GOES MY HOPE OF 'PHONING FOR HELP!

GLAD THEY DIDN'T BOTHER WITH THIS CUPBOARD! I HAD A SQUINT IN HERE WHEN WE FIRST CAME. COMMANDANT'S GAS MASK AND A FEW TEAR-GAS BOMBS FOR STOPPING RIOTS.

I CAN'T STOP THAT LOT! BEST WAIT TILL THEY'RE GONE THEN HAVE A GO AT THEIR BLOKES LEFT BEHIND TO GUARD OUR GUARDS.

Some minutes later —
ACHTUNG! POISON GAS!
TRY A WHIFF OF PHOSGENE, CHUMS!

GAD! TEAR-GAS SMOKE!
DON'T TELL THE JERRIES, SIR! THEY THINK IT'S POISON GAS.

LIEUTENANT BATES IS IN THERE. KNOCKED OUT BY THOSE HUN SWINE WHEN THEY DISARMED OUR GUARDS.
SEEMS HE TRIED TO MAKE A FIGHT OF IT, ANYWAY! HOW ABOUT THE ARMOURY HUT?

THE JERRIES DIDN'T BOTHER WITH OUR SPARE WEAPONS. THEY HAD MORE THAN ENOUGH OF THER OWN.
ARMOURY
SO LET'S GO AFTER 'EM!

BUT WHICH WAY DID THEY GO TOWARDS THE FRONT?
I HEARD THEIR OFFICER TALKING ABOUT THE RAILWAY SIDING NEAR THIS CAMP.

GAD! THE BLIGHTERS ARE TAKING A SUPPLY TRAIN!
SEE 'EM OFF, LADS!

IT'S TOO RISKY TO TAKE THE WHOLE TRAIN NOW. A STRAY BULLET COULD BLOW UP THE AMMUNITION. JUST HOLD OFF THE TOMMIES UNTIL WE GET THIS TANK UNLOADED. IT WILL ADD SOME WEIGHT TO OUR ATTACK BEHIND THE BRITISH FRONT LINES.

THEY'RE RUNNING FROM US, CORP!
ONLY BECAUSE THEY'VE SWIPED THAT TANK!

NOT MUCH WE CAN DO TO STOP THAT NOW!
WE'LL HAVE TO TRY, SIR, OR YOU'LL HAVE SOME AWKWARD QUESTIONS TO ANSWER AT A COURT-MARTIAL ENQUIRY!

THE JERRIES MUST HAVE CHASED OFF THE ENGINE CREW. BUT IT'S GOT STEAM UP, SO WE'LL USE THE TRAIN TO CATCH UP WITH 'EM.
THEN WHAT? FIGHT A TANK WITH RIFLES?

THE HUNS ARE BOUND TO SPOT US COMING!

THE TANK'S FIRING! ONE HIT ON THESE AMMUNITION TRUCKS COULD BLOW US SKY-HIGH!

HOP OFF, LADS! BIT OF A BUMP COMING!
GAD, NO! YOU CAN'T MEAN TO RAM IT?

AAAGH!

FEUER!
NIP OFF UNDER COVER OF THE STEAM.
URH!

I DOUBT IF WE CAN HANDLE ALL THOSE JERRIES EVEN WITHOUT THEIR TANK!
HOW ABOUT THIS GUN AMMO, SARGE?

YOU GONE MAD, CORP? TRYING TO SET OFF THOSE SHELLS?
THEY'RE NOT FUSED FOR EXPLOSIVES YET. GET YOUR LADS TO OPEN THE NOSE CONES!

HIMMEL! THE TOMMIES HAVE SET OFF GAS SHELLS.
GET CLEAR!

YOU IDIOT, SMITH! SOME OF IT'S DRIFTING BACK ON US! GIVE ME THAT MASK!

RUN!
THOSE JERRIES ARE FRONT-LINE TROOPS. THEY'RE SO SCARED OF GAS THEY DON'T WAIT TO SPOT WE ONLY SET OFF SMOKE-SCREEN SHELLS! I GOT THE IDEA FROM THAT TEAR GAS LARK BACK AT THE CAMP.
EH? WHAT? ONLY SMOKE?

Next day, at a brigade HQ —
SO ALL THOSE HUNS WERE SOON ROUNDED UP, BRIGADIER?
YES, THANKS TO THE WAY YOU PANICKED THEM WITH THAT FAKE GAS ATTACK, CAPTAIN.

THE ENEMY ATTACK ON OUR FRONT HERE WAS HALTED, TOO, BUT IT MIGHT HAVE SUCCEEDED IF THOSE GERMANS HAD ARRIVED ON OUR REAR WITH THAT HEAVY TANK. YOU DESERVE ANOTHER MEDAL!
MERELY DOING MY DUTY AS USUAL.

SO IT IS BACK TO THE PRISON CAMP, SIR?
NO, SMITH, TO PARIS FOR A SPOT OF WELL-EARNED LEAVE.

YOU WILL, OF COURSE, RETURN TO THE FRONT AFTER DROPPING ME OFF AT THE RAIL STATION.
SUITS ME! THIS BLINKING WAR'S BAD ENOUGH WITHOUT HAVING TO GO ON LEAVE WITH OUR HERO HERE, TOO!
The End

Fight To A Finish!

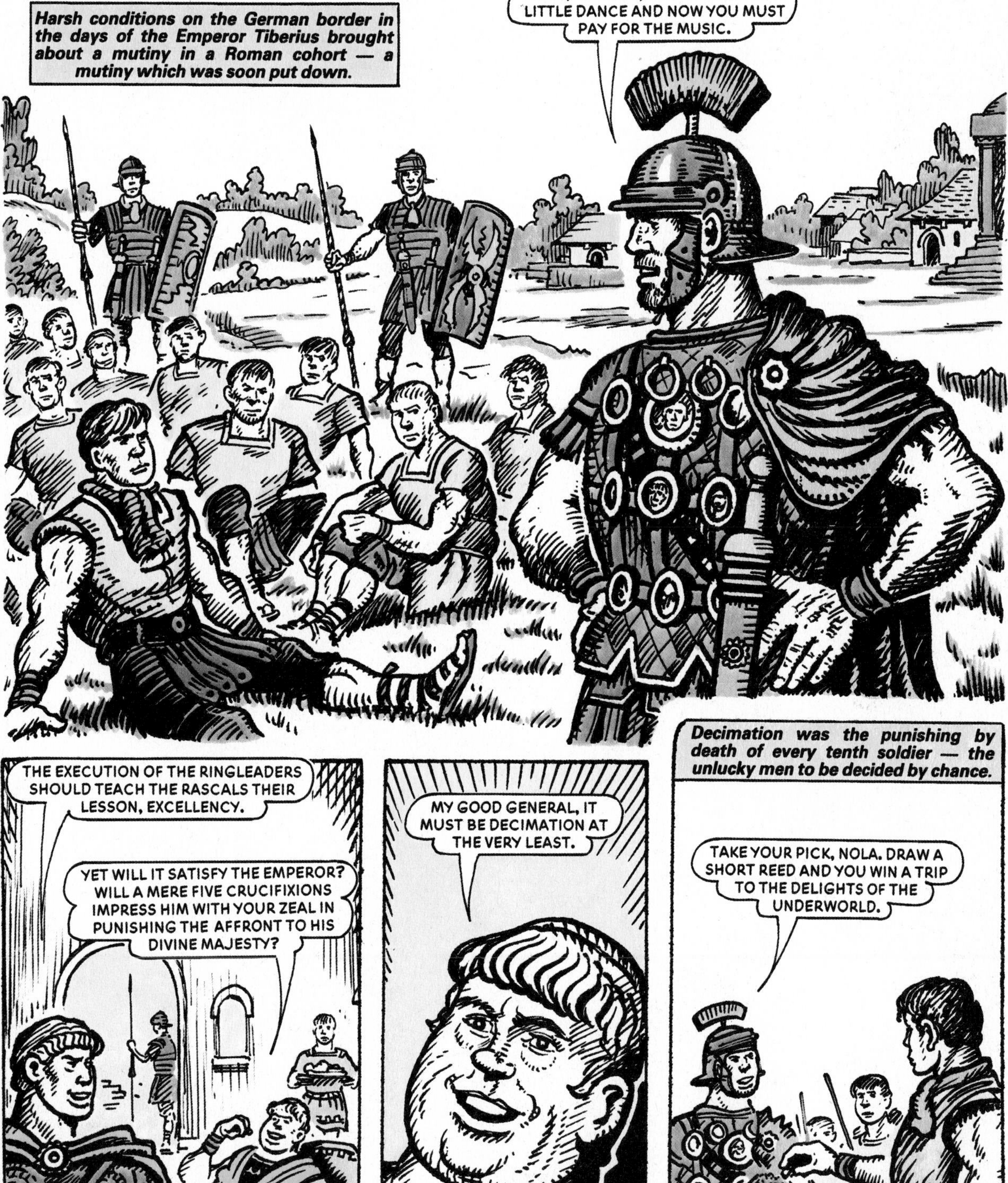

Harsh conditions on the German border in the days of the Emperor Tiberius brought about a mutiny in a Roman cohort — a mutiny which was soon put down.
WELL, MY LADS, YOU'VE HAD YOUR LITTLE DANCE AND NOW YOU MUST PAY FOR THE MUSIC.
THE EXECUTION OF THE RINGLEADERS SHOULD TEACH THE RASCALS THEIR LESSON, EXCELLENCY.
YET WILL IT SATISFY THE EMPEROR? WILL A MERE FIVE CRUCIFIXIONS IMPRESS HIM WITH YOUR ZEAL IN PUNISHING THE AFFRONT TO HIS DIVINE MAJESTY?
MY GOOD GENERAL, IT MUST BE DECIMATION AT THE VERY LEAST.
Decimation was the punishing by death of every tenth soldier — the unlucky men to be decided by chance.
TAKE YOUR PICK, NOLA. DRAW A SHORT REED AND YOU WIN A TRIP TO THE DELIGHTS OF THE UNDERWORLD.

SHORT IT IS. NOLA, I'M SORRY TO LOSE A GOOD SOLDIER LIKE YOU, BUT THE GODS HAVE DECIDED.
The chosen sixty were brought together—
NOLA, THIS LOOKS LIKE A FAMILY MEETING. THERE IS YOUR YOUNG BROTHER.
HE HAS THE FAMILY LUCK, MAGNUS.
WELL, BROTHER, WE CAME INTO THE WORLD TWO YEARS APART, BUT IT LOOKS LIKE WE'LL LEAVE IT TOGETHER.
YOUNG 'UN, I'LL PROVE MY AFFECTION BY FORGETTING THOSE FIVE SESTERCES YOU OWE ME.
LADS, YOU ARE IN LUCK. THE NOBLE GOVERNOR HAS PREVAILED ON THE GENERAL NOT TO NAIL YOU TO CROSSES. INSTEAD, YOU WILL GO OUT LIKE SOLDIERS OF ROME — FIGHTING!
THE FIGHTING WILL BE AMONG YOURSELVES. YOU FIGHT TO THE DEATH. AS ENCOURAGEMENT FOR A GOOD SHOW, HIS EXCELLENCY WISHES IT TO BE KNOWN THAT A PARDON WILL BE GRANTED TO THE MAN WHO OUTLIVES THE REST.
The doomed men were marched out—
SMARTEN THAT STEP. ON MY COMMAND, YOU WILL BRISKLY PICK UP WEAPONS AND FORM INTO TWO FACING TEAMS.

EXCELLENCY, THOSE WHO ARE ABOUT TO DIE SALUTE YOU.
YOU HAVE MY PERMISSION TO START THE PROCEEDINGS.

SO MUCH MORE PLEASANT THIS WAY, MY DEAR GENERAL. EXECUTIONS CAN BE SUCH TEDIOUS AFFAIRS.

A NICE, LOUD, LOYAL CHEER, MY LADS. THEN YOU CAN GET STUCK IN.

HAIL CAESAR! HAIL!

Then the javelins flew—
ARGH!

The teams charged—
STICK CLOSE TO ME, YOUNG 'UN.
RIGHT, OLD 'UN. THE REST FIGHT FOR THEMSELVES, BUT WE WATCH FOR EACH OTHER.

THOSE TWO FELLOWS APPEAR TO BE WORKING AS A TEAM.

TWO BROTHERS FROM ISTRIA. GOOD SOLDIERS.

Then there were only three men left alive—

SO NOW IT'S ME AGAINST YOU AND YOUR LITTLE BROTHER, NOLA.

IT'S GOOD TO END AMONG OLD FRIENDS, MAGNUS.

DIDN'T WE COME TOGETHER IN THAT LITTLE FROLIC AGAINST THE SWISSERS TEN YEARS BACK?

SO WE DID. IN THE HIGH ALPS THAT CHILL WINTER.

URNH!
MAY THE GODS BE GOOD TO YOU, OLD FRIEND!

THE TWO BROTHERS ARE LEFT, BUT ONLY ONE MAY SURVIVE. THIS REALLY IS DELIGHTFULLY ENTERTAINING.

TEN GOLD PIECES SAY THE OLDER BROTHER WINS!
A GOOD WAGER. I'LL TAKE THE YOUNGER MAN TO WIN!
DON'T HOLD BACK, OLD 'UN!
YOUNG 'UN, YOU MAY COUNT ON ME.

Nola struck—

HE MADE NO ATTEMPT TO DEFEND HIMSELF. MOST DISAPPOINTING.
ARGH!

THE PUNISHMENT IS COMPLETE. HIS EXCELLENCY GRACIOUSLY RESTORES TO DUTY THE ONE SURVIVOR.

Nola was called forward—

SOLDIER, ONE DETAIL INTRIGUES ME. WHY DID YOUR BROTHER ALLOW YOU TO KILL HIM?
LORD, WE HAD CAST DICE TO DECIDE WHICH OF US SHOULD LIVE IF THE CHANCE CAME.

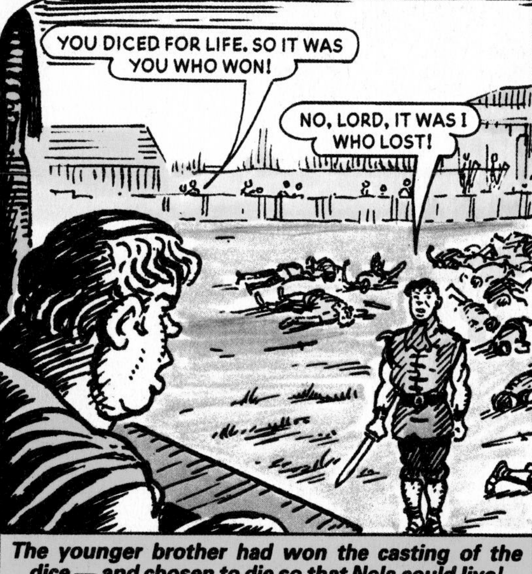
YOU DICED FOR LIFE. SO IT WAS YOU WHO WON!
NO, LORD, IT WAS I WHO LOST!

The younger brother had won the casting of the dice — and chosen to die so that Nola could live!

VICTOR Sports Crossword

CLUES DOWN

1. A good one can lead to a goal. (5)
2. Get your skates on if you want to enjoy yourself here. (3, 4)
3. This girl javelin thrower is a bit backward at first. (5)
4. An away match can give you a good one. (6)
5. One of England's most famous batsmen. (7)
6. A Royal racecourse. (5)
7. This football team suits a lot of Edinburgh fans. (6)
13. Is this side a bit bottom heavy? (6)
14. Most games do this in the second half. (7)
16. ------- Bembridge, a famous British golfer. (7)
17. He has a lot of fishy stories. (6)
19. This 'Kidd' is an old hand a stunt riding! (5)
21. He became undisputed heavyweight champion of the world in 1987. (5)
22. Scoring ones are very important in cricket. (5)

CLUES ACROSS

1 and 5. An American football player who would certainly growl! (7,4.)
8. They are limited in one day cricket. (5)
9. You get four points for one in rugby. (3)
10. One of Britain's greatest-ever middle-distance runners. (3)
11. An England 'keeper for many years. (7)
12. Next to an inner on an archery target. (5.)
13. They motor — or pedal! (6)
15. When they are drawn, play is over. (6)
18. This town has a football team and a test cricket ground. (5)
20. A long distance runner from Scotland. (3, 4)
23. This sort won't fly very far over the links. (3, 4)
24. The ----- and Greavsie, a well-known TV team. (5)
25. All athletes wear one. (4)
26. Glasgow has them — and so does Berwick! (7)

ANSWERS ON PAGE 75

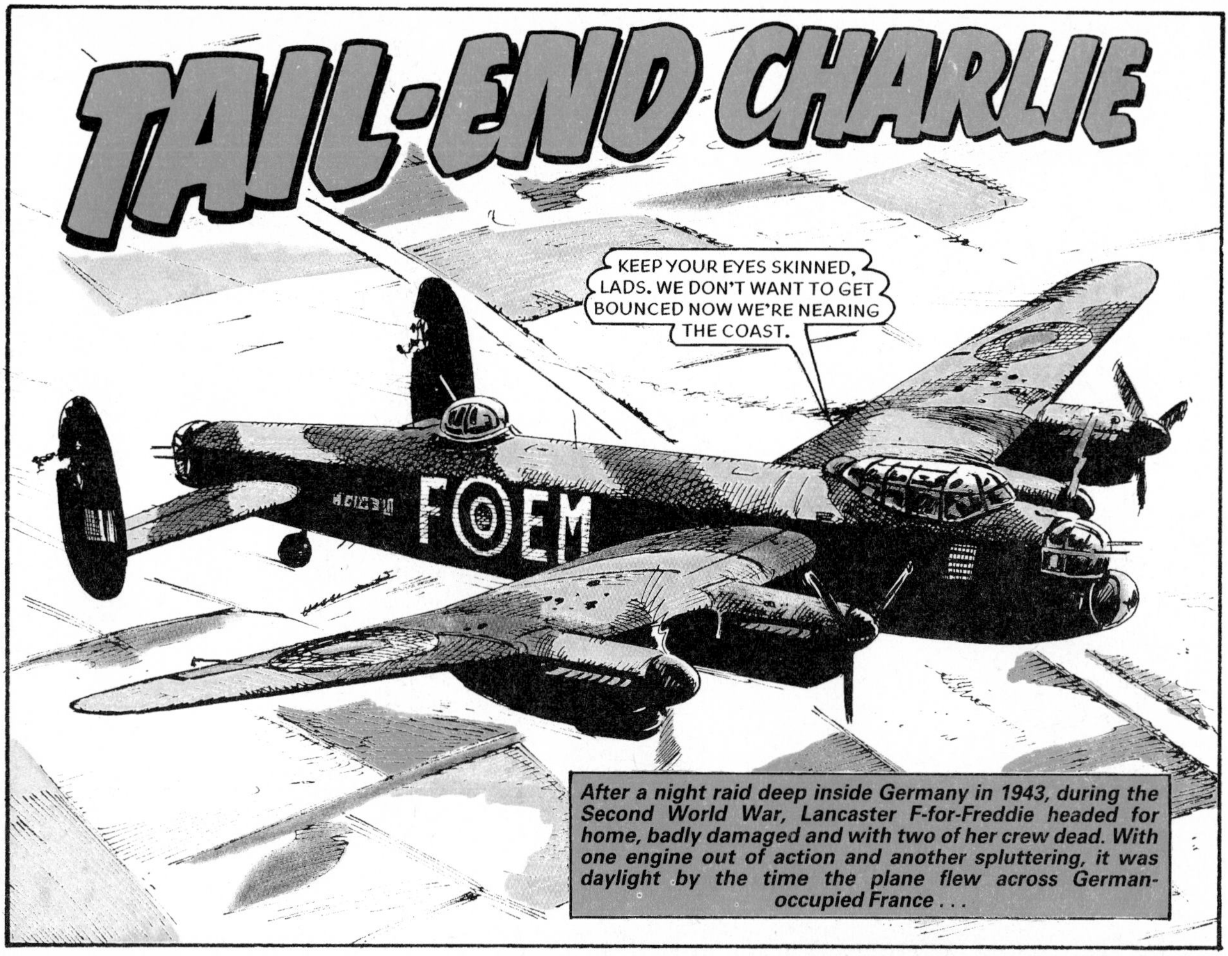

TAIL-END CHARLIE

KEEP YOUR EYES SKINNED, LADS. WE DON'T WANT TO GET BOUNCED NOW WE'RE NEARING THE COAST.

F-EM

After a night raid deep inside Germany in 1943, during the Second World War, Lancaster F-for-Freddie headed for home, badly damaged and with two of her crew dead. With one engine out of action and another spluttering, it was daylight by the time the plane flew across German-occupied France . . .

But their luck was out. In the rear turrec their most experienced gunner, Sergeant Charlie Lucas, known as "Tail-End Charlie" to the rest of the crew, was the first to spot the enemy plane —

BANDIT AT FIVE O'CLOCK! A FOCKE-WULF 190!

YOU WILL NEVER REACH HOME, BRITISHERS!

Cannon shells ripped apart the Lancaster's rear turret—
AARGH!

COR, THE CANOPY'S DISAPPEARED! BUT THE GUNS ARE STILL INTACT AND SO AM I — MORE OR LESS!

HERE HE COMES AGAIN!

IT'S YOU OR ME, FRITZ!

GOT HIM!
GOOD SHOOTING, CHARLIE!

NOW BOTH PORT ENGINES HAVE GONE! WE'RE NOT GOING TO MAKE IT! I'LL PUT HER DOWN! WE'RE TOO LOW TO BALE OUT NOW!

HANG ON TO YOUR HATS, LADS! AND GET CLEAR AS SOON AS WE'RE DOWN!

THERE SHE GOES!
ONLY FOUR OF US, SKIPPER?
JOE DIDN'T GET CLEAR IN TIME AND PETE AND BILL HAD ALREADY BOUGHT IT!
WHAT'S BEST NOW, CHARLIE?
LET'S GET AS FAR AWAY FROM HERE AS WE CAN, FOR A START!

It was natural for the young skipper, Flying Officer Tony Brent, to ask Charlie for advice, for the experienced tail-gunner had been shot down before and escaped from Occupied Europe. After walking across country for half an hour the British fliers were clear of the immediate vicinity of their crash-landing, and Charlie laid his plans. So it was that Private Hans Lubeck of the German Army came to see a body lying in the road as he drove his stores truck along it . . .

WHAT'S THIS?

BETTER BE CAREFUL.

AAGH!

Charlie quickly donned the German's tunic and cap.
WHERE TO NOW, CHARLIE? THE COAST?
NO, SKIPPER, WE'LL HEAD INLAND. THAT'S THE LAST THING THE JERRIES WILL EXPECT AND IT'LL GIVE US A BREATHING SPACE TO TRY TO CONTACT THE RESISTANCE.

THAT LOT WILL BE LOOKING FOR US. I HOPE THE LADS KEEP THEIR HEADS DOWN IN THE BACK.

Later —
HEY, THAT MONUMENT ON THE HILL LOOKS FAMILIAR! I'VE SEEN THAT BEFORE!

Charlie quickly stopped the truck.
WHY HAVE YOU STOPPED, CHARLIE?
I'VE JUST REALISED WHERE WE ARE! IN 1940 I WAS STATIONED FOR A FEW WEEKS AT AN AIRFIELD AT ACHTINGER, ON THE OTHER SIDE OF THAT HILL, UNTIL THE JERRIES DROVE US OUT.

AND THE AIRFIELD WILL STILL BE THERE! WE MIGHT HAVE A CHANCE TO PINCH A PLANE!
WELL, THE PERIMETER FENCE WON'T KEEP US OUT, UNLESS THEY'VE STRENGTHENED IT! WE'LL BE ABLE TO SEE THE FIELD FROM THE HILL.

NEARLY THERE. TIME TO GET RID OF THIS JERRY UNIFORM — AND THE TRUCK.

Minutes later —
NO POINT IN LEAVING IT FOR THE HUN!

And soon —
THEY HAVEN'T STRENGTHENED THE FENCE. AND THAT FIESELER STORCH WOULD DO US, ESPECIALLY AS THEY'RE REFUELLING IT. HOW ABOUT IT SKIPPER?
I RECKON I COULD FLY IT ALL RIGHT. WE'LL WAIT HERE TILL DARK AND MAKE OUR PLANS MEANWHILE.

After dark —
QUIETLY NOW. THERE'S A SENTRY NEAR THE FOCKE-WULF! I'LL FIX HIM WHILE YOU HEAD FOR THE STORCH.

THAT'S IT, CHUM. YOU THINK OF YOUR NEXT LEAVE.

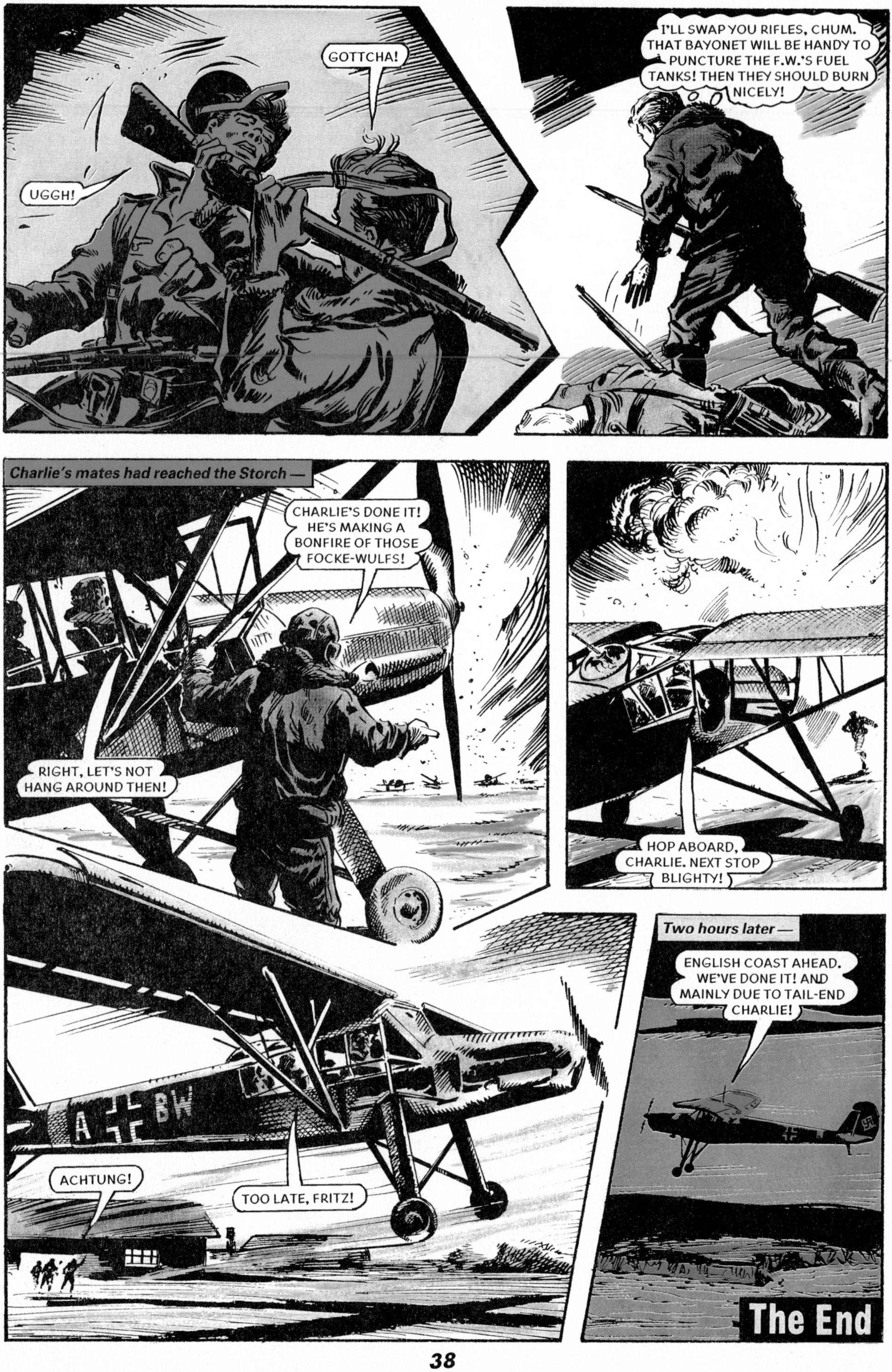

Charlie's mates had reached the Storch —

CHARLIE'S DONE IT! HE'S MAKING A BONFIRE OF THOSE FOCKE-WULFS!

RIGHT, LET'S NOT HANG AROUND THEN!

HOP ABOARD, CHARLIE. NEXT STOP BLIGHTY!

ACHTUNG!

TOO LATE, FRITZ!

Two hours later —

ENGLISH COAST AHEAD. WE'VE DONE IT! AND MAINLY DUE TO TAIL-END CHARLIE!

The End

A TALE OF TWO STARS

MY NAME IS BILL POWELL AND I'M CHIEF SCOUT FOR FIRST DIVISION BURNHAM CITY. BURNHAM HAVE BEEN ONE OF THE COUNTRY'S TOP TEAMS FOR SOME YEARS NOW, AND A LOT OF THE CREDIT FOR THAT IS DUE TO OUR CAST-IRON DEFENCE, ESPECIALLY OUR CAPTAIN AND CENTRE-HALF SAM HORTON, AND OUR ENGLAND INTERNATIONAL GOALKEEPER, BOBBY BLYTH. MIND YOU, BOBBY LOOKED AS IF HE WAS GOING TO BE A FAILURE AT ONE TIME . . .

Six years ago Bobby was just a promising kid in the third team. It was the day before our first team was due to play the Scottish club Dunaber United in the U.E.F.A. Cup, and I was chatting to our manager, John Freeman, when —
BAD NEWS, BOSS! LES GRAHAM, THE RESERVE KEEPER, WAS RUSHED INTO HOSPITAL LAST NIGHT WITH APPENDICITIS!
MANAGER
YES, HE HAD AN OPERATION THIS MORNING, JOE — HE'S OKAY BUT IT MEANS WE'LL HAVE TO FIND ALTERNATIVE GOALKEEPER COVER FOR TOMORROW. I THOUGHT WE MIGHT PROMOTE YOUNG BOBBY BLYTH FROM THE THIRD TEAM.

I THOUGHT HE WAS A GREAT PROSPECT WHEN I SIGNED HIM, JOHN, BUT HE'S NEVER PLAYED BEFORE MORE THAN A HANDFUL OF SPECTATORS. IT'D BE LIKE CHUCKING HIM IN AT THE DEEP END WITHOUT KNOWING IF HE CAN SWIM!
HE'LL HAVE TO LEARN SOME TIME. ANYWAY, JUST TO BE ON THE BENCH'D GIVE HIM A TASTE OF THE BIG-TIME — I DOUBT IF WE'LL ACTUALLY HAVE TO USE HIM, SO WE'LL RISK IT!

For Bobby Blyth, Wednesday was the most awesome day of his life. It was the second leg of the U.E.F.A. Cup-tie, the first leg having been drawn 1-1.
WHAT'S ALL THIS, LAD — NOT NERVOUS, SURELY? DON'T BE — YOU'RE JUST ALONG FOR THE RIDE SO RELAX AND ENJOY IT.
D-DON'T WORRY ABOUT ME, JOE — I'LL BE ALL RIGHT ONCE I'M OUT THERE!

But at the first, ear-shattering roar of the crowd —
RAAAAAAAH!
OH, NO . . . !
WELL, DON'T JUST STAND THERE, SON — YOU'RE MAKING THE PLACE LOOK UNTIDY!

A-ALL THOSE PEOPLE, BOSS! THE-THE NOISE! I-I CAN'T FACE IT . . . LOOK, I-I'LL GO BACK AND WAIT IN THE DRESSING-ROOM . . .
YOU'LL DO NO SUCH THING. GET HOLD OF YOURSELF, LAD, FOR PETE'S SAKE! JOE, GRAB HIS OTHER ARM AND LET'S GET HIM TO THE DUG-OUT!

TH-THEY'RE LIKE A LOT OF ANIMALS BAYING FOR BLOOD — IT COULD BE MINE!
CITY! CITY! RAAAH!
THE POOR LAD'S HAVING KITTENS — I HOPE TO HECK WE DON'T HAVE TO SEND HIM ON!

Play was scrappy for most of the first half.
GET HOLD OF YOURSELVES, CITY!

Then, ten minutes before half-time . . .
THEY'RE THROUGH — OUT, KEEPER, OUT . . . !

GOSH, SORRY, PAL!
AAGH!

SOON HAVE YOU FIXED UP, PETE, MATE — THE TRAINER'S ON HIS WAY!
IT WASN'T DELIBERATE, REF, HONEST — I COULDN'T PULL BACK IN TIME, THAT'S ALL!

JUST GIVE ME A SQUIRT OF THE OLD PAIN-KILLER, JOE. I-I'LL BE OKAY . . .
NOT THIS TIME, SON. YOU'VE GOT A BUSTED RIB THERE, IF NOT TWO — IT'S THE HOSPITAL FOR YOU!

The moment Bobby dreaded had arrived!
RIGHT, LET'S HAVE YOU, BOBBY — YOU'RE ON!
I-I CAN'T, BOSS, I JUST CAN'T!

YOU CAN AND YOU WILL, MY SON, IF I HAVE TO CARRY YOU ALL THE WAY ACROSS THERE PERSONALLY! SHOVE HIM OUT OF THERE, THE REST OF YOU!
ALL RIGHT, ALL RIGHT, I-I'M GOING . . . !

NERVOUS, KID?
P-P-PETRIFIED!
DON'T WORRY, SON — YOU'LL BE OKAY ONCE YOU'VE GOT A COUPLE OF SAVES UNDER YOUR BELT!

IS HIS NAME BOBBY OR JELLY? THE WAY HE'S SHAKING MAKES YOU WONDER. AND HERE COME UNITED!
UNITED! UNITED!

YEEEES-GOOAAL!
STONE THE CROWS, HE'S WORSE THAN I THOUGHT — HADN'T A BLOOMIN' CLUE!
JUST CLOSED HIS EYES AND FLAPPED LIKE A DEMENTED DUCK!

Bobby floundered helplessly as United piled on the pressure.

THAT LAD'S A NERVOUS WRECK, BILL, BUT THERE MUST BE SOME WAY WE CAN PULL HIM TOGETHER — ANY IDEAS?
THERE'S JUST ONE POSSIBILITY, JOHN. I'LL GO ON DOWN TO THE TREATMENT ROOM — SEND BOBBY IN AS SOON AS HE COMES OFF!

A few minutes later it was half-time . . .
BOSS, I KNOW I'VE LET EVERYONE DOWN AND I COULDN'T GO THROUGH THAT AGAIN, EVER. SO I'M GIVING UP FOOTBALL, RIGHT NOW!
TREATMENT ROOM
I THINK BILL POWELL MAY HAVE A BETTER SOLUTION, LAD. HE'S WAITING FOR YOU IN THE TREATMENT ROOM NOW, SO OFF YOU GO!

SORRY TO SAY IT, BOSS, BUT THAT KID HASN'T GOT WHAT IT TAKES — A KEEPER NEEDS NERVE, NOT NERVES!
I'M INCLINED TO AGREE, SAM, SO YOU'D BETTER BE PREPARED FOR ANYTHING — ONE OF YOU MAY YET FINISH UP IN GOAL TODAY!

Ten minutes later . . .
BILL POWELL'S SURE TAKING HIS TIME IN THERE. BETTER TAKE THE OTHERS OUT, SAM, WHILE I STIR THINGS UP!
OK, BOSS. COME ON, LADS.

SO THERE YOU ARE. WHAT . . . ?
IT'S OK, JOHN — OFF YOU GO, SON!

WELL, IS HE GOING TO BE ALL RIGHT?
I HONESTLY DON'T KNOW, JOHN — LET'S KEEP OUR FINGERS CROSSED AND HOPE FOR THE BEST, SHALL WE?
United attacked from the restart —
THEY'RE THROUGH AGAIN — MUST SCORE . . . NOTHING TO STOP THEM, IS THERE?
UNITED! UNITED! RAAAH!
But this time —
OOOOOOH!
WELL, WHADDYA KNOW! GREAT SAVE!
Bobby began to play brilliantly.
Then —
WELL USED! THAT KID'S A REVELATION, BILL — WHAT ON EARTH DID YOU DO TO HIM?
NEVER MIND THAT NOW, JOHN. WE COULD BE ON TO SOMETHING HERE!
GREAT GOAL! WE'RE LEVEL NOW!
YEH, BUT THE THROW STARTED IT — THAT KID'S NO MUG AFTER ALL!
And five minutes later —
GOAL! CITY! CITY!
A win for City seemed certain until, in the closing minutes —
FOUL, REF — PENALTY!!

But again Bobby turned up trumps!

And so the match was won.

BOBBY BLYTH! BOBBY BLYTH!
YOU DESERVE THOSE CHEERS, SON — I'M PROUD OF YOU! BUT TELL ME BILL, JUST WHAT DID YOU DO TO HIM AT HALF-TIME?
SHOW HIM, BOBBY!

EAR-PLUGS — OF COURSE! NOW WHY DIDN'T I THINK OF THAT?
IT WAS THE VOLUME THAT UNNERVED ME, BOSS. ONCE IT WAS SHUT OFF I WAS ABLE TO FORGET THE CROWD AND PLAY MY NATURAL GAME. THE WAY IT SOUNDS NOW, THOUGH, I THINK I'M GOING TO LIKE IT!

AND BOBBY DID GET TO LIKE THE ROAR OF THE CROWD. HE NEVER NEEDED EAR-PLUGS AGAIN AND NOW HE'S AN ENGLAND REGULAR. BIG SAM HORTON'S AN ENGLAND PLAYER TOO, AND THE MOST DEPENDABLE CENTRE-HALF I'VE EVER SEEN — EXCEPT, THAT IS, FOR ONE STRANGE GAME, A GAME IN WHICH HE ACTUALLY SCORED FIVE GOALS!

It was a couple of years ago and we were away to Donnington Rovers in a vital league game.

Big Sam ruled the middle of the park.

THE ROVERS' STRIKERS WON'T GET MUCH JOY TODAY!

And in City's most desperate moments . . .

WELL DONE, SAM!

Then —
YEUK!
GREAT BALL, SAM!
CORNER, REF!
I'VE SEEN YOU, SAM — FAR POST IT IS!
NUTS! HORTON'S SCORED!
Shortly before half-time . . .
TAKE IT, SAM!
EVERYBODY'S COVERED, SO LET'S HAVE A BASH AT THE UNEXPECTED!
WOW, WHAT A CRACKER — ALL OF 35 YARDS!
GOOAAAL!

At half-time City still led 2-0
SAM HORTON! SUPER SAM!
LISTEN TO THAT, SAM — WHAT DOES IT FEEL LIKE TO BE A STAR?
AH, THAT'S JUST FOR NOW, PAL — A COUPLE OF MISTAKES IN THE SECOND HALF AND THEY'LL BE BOOING ME OFF THE PARK. I JUST TRY NOT TO LET IT BOTHER ME, EITHER WAY!

Rovers came back full of determination . . .
AH, THIS LOOKS A BIT MORE PROMISING! BUT THEY'VE STILL GOT TO FIND A WAY AROUND HORTON!

But Sam's domination still seemed complete —

YOU DON'T KNOW WHICH WAY TO GO, DO YOU, CHUM?

OH, YES, I DO!

Sam had been conned!

YOUR BALL, PETE!

MY BALL!

OH, NO!

IT'S THERE - GOAAAL!

MADE A RIGHT PIG'S EAR OF THAT, DIDN'T YOU? IT WAS MY SHOUT AND MY BALL!
A MISUNDERSTANDING, BOBBY — OK? IT WON'T HAPPEN AGAIN!
But Rovers were forcing the pace now —
WELL PLAYED, BOBBY. STEADY NOW, LADS — MARK 'EM TIGHT AND LET'S NOT HAVE ANY MISTAKES!
Again Fate took a hand —
OOOOOPH!
YEUK!
YOU DID IT AGAIN — I HAD IT COVERED!
I WAS BARGED IN THE BACK, FOR PETE'S SAKE — IT'S HARDLY MY FAULT THAT THE REF'S BLIND! DON'T WORRY, THERE'S PLENTY OF TIME — WE'LL GET IT BACK!
But Rovers' luck held, despite Sam's efforts . . .
Then, with time running out —
PENALTY, REF!
PHEEEP!

BETTER LET ME TAKE IT, SAM — IT'S BEEN MY JOB ALL SEASON AND I'VE NOT MISSED ONE YET!

WELL, EVERYONE MISSES SOMETIME, PAL, AND IT COULD BE YOUR TURN TODAY, SO I'LL TAKE IT MYSELF TO BE ON THE SAFE SIDE.

HE'S MISSED IT!

A RIGHT MESS I MADE OF THAT! IT'LL BE EVEN WORSE IF THEY SCORE FROM THIS — MUST GET BACK TO GIVE COVER!

I CAN HANDLE IT, SAM! KEEP AWAY FOR PETE'S SAKE!

YEUK!

OH, NO — NOT AGAIN!

Sure enough, the jinx struck again!

WALLY'S ISLAND
The South Pacific during the Second World War, and the crew of the Royal Navy destroyer Tearaway found time to remember a lost shipmate.
THIS IS ABOUT WHERE HE WENT OVER, SIR.
I'M GLAD WE'VE FINALLY PASSED THIS WAY AGAIN, NUMBER ONE. MUSTER THE OFF-WATCH HANDS.
SHIP'S COMPANY, WE ARE GATHERED TO PAY HOMAGE TO THE MEMORY OF A SHIPMATE LOST OVERBOARD IN THAT STORM LAST YEAR. I REFER TO ABLE SEAMAN WALTER POTTS, GENERALLY KNOWN AS WALLY — A USEFUL HAND APART FROM A TALENT FOR TRIPPING OVER HIS OWN FEET.
While on an island not a hundred miles away—
WOTCHER, WALLY MATE!
LOVELY DAY, POKO. MY REGARDS TO THE FAMILY.
JUST A FISTFUL MORE BREADFRUIT THICKENING, I RECKON, MUM. I LIKES MY FISH STEW A BIT STIFF.
GOOD, MATE. I DO.

CAST UP TO ROUGH IT AMONG PRIMITIVE FOLKS WHILE ME LUCKY SHIPMATES GET ON WITH THE WAR! LIFE CAN BE HARD AND CRUEL!

Wally's rough life was suddenly interrupted.
WALLY MATE! GREAT IRON CANOE COME.
HUM! YANK OR BRITISH, I WONDER?

BLIMEY! IT'S A JAP SUB.
SHE'S DROPPING HER HOOK! MATIES, IT'S ME FOR THE MANGROVES!

WALLY, WE HELP YOU FIGHT THEM BAD BLOKES.
POKO, AIN'T MY SCHOOLING LEARNED YOU LOT NOTHING? YOUR BEST BET IS TO TREAT THE NIPS POLITE AND RESPECTFUL.

Wally headed for the interior swamps.
COULD BE JUST FOR REPAIRS OR TO TAKE ON WATER. MAYBE THAT NIP'LL BE GONE BY TOMORROW.

Imperial Navy Captain Ishigami had other ideas.
A DEEPWATER LAGOON ACCORDING TO THE SOUNDINGS ON THIS BRITISH NAVY CHART — ONE SMALL NATIVE VILLAGE DETECTED BY OUR OWN AERIAL SURVEY. AN IDEAL SECRET BASE FOR STRIKES AGAINST ALLIED CONVOYS.

ORDINARY SEAMAN SAWADA, DO UP THAT FLAPPING GAITER, YOU HORRIBLE PERSON!
CERTAINLY — AT ONCE, CHIEF!

Wally was informed of events over the next two days.
JAPONI BLOKES SAY PEOPLE WORK OR BE PUNISHED. THEY MAKE US CUT TREES FOR MAKE BIG RAFT.

A RAFT? HUM! THE NIPS MUST BE PLANNING TO UNLOAD SUPPLIES.

Wally prowled by night.
A RAFT THIS SIZE MEANS A LOT OF UNLOADING. CRIPES! THE CHEEKY SWABS MUST INTEND USING MY ISLAND AS A BASE.

A BEACH PATROL!

WHY'S HE STOPPED? BLIMEY, I THINK HE'S STRIKING A MATCH.

JUST MY LUCK — A NIP OUT FOR A CRAFTY DRAG, AND HE'S SPOTTED ME!

Wally moved quickly.
AT LEAST I'VE GOT BACCY AND MATCHES OUT OF IT. HAVEN'T HAD A PUFF AT MY OLD PIPE SINCE I GOT WASHED OFF THE TEARAWAY.
Next morning—
SIR, IT WAS NO NATIVE, BUT A WHITE MAN WITH AN UGLY RED FACE AND GLARING ROUND EYES.
SIX STROKES OF THE CANE FOR FAILING IN YOUR DUTY. MARCH HIM OFF.
THE NATIVES CLAIM TO KNOW NOTHING, BUT PETTY OFFICER HAYASHI FOUND TRACKS THAT MATCH THOSE ON THE BEACH AND LEAD INTO THE SWAMP.
THE INTRUDER MUST BE LOCATED. HE COULD BE AN ENEMY COASTWATCHER — WHICH MEANS A WIRELESS TRANSMITTER AND THE END OF THE SECRECY WE NEED.
A patrol was sent out—
HORRIBLE SEAMAN SAWADA, I CHOSE YOU ONLY BECAUSE I MAY HAVE NEED OF AN INTERPRETER TO TALK TO THIS BARBARIAN — BUT COME NEAR JABBING ME JUST ONCE MORE WITH YOUR BAYONET AND I SHALL STAMP YOU INTO THIS MUD!
SO VERY SORRY, CHIEF. I HUMBLY BEG PARDON.
IT AIN'T BUTTERFLIES THEM JAPS IS AFTER. I OUGHT TO HOP IT FAST.
BUT BLOWED IF I WILL. IT'S ABOUT TIME THAT SLANT-EYED LOT LEARNED THIS IS MY ISLAND.

The patrol sighted smoke.
SMOKE, CHIEF.
I SEE IT, HORRIBLE SEAMAN. I SEE ALSO WE ARE BACK ON THE LINE OF FOOTPRINTS AND THEY LEAD TOWARDS THAT SAME SMOKE.
EXTEND IN SKIRMISHING ORDER. FORWARD — ADVANCE!
The patrol marched into muddy trouble.
QUAGMIRE! PULL BACK!
THAT LITTLE 'UN'S IN THE WORST BIT OF MUDHOLE. LOOKS LIKE HE'S HAD IT.
WHY AM I DOING THIS? I MUST BE OFF ME BLOOMING ROCKER.
SAVED BY AN ENEMY! THIS IS MOST AWKWARD.
HEY, YOU! COP HOLD!
THANK YOU! MOST KINDLY!

The muddy patrol fell back to the beach.
THERE ARE OTHER WAYS OF HUNTING A PREY. CHIEF, SELECT TEN MEN OF THE VILLAGE.

Later that day—
YOU LISTEN! YOU SURRENDER OR NATIVE MEN BE KILLED. YOU LISTEN!
OH NO!

EITHER HE DOES NOT HEAR OR HE DOES NOT BELIEVE. PETTY OFFICER. STRIKE OFF THE OLD MAN'S HEAD.

PETTY OFFICER, DO NOT STRIKE OFF THE OLD MAN'S HEAD!
WAIT! HE COMES!

CAPTAIN SALUTE BRAVE MAN. HE ASK IF YOU WISH DIE NOW OR PREFER WAIT TILL RISE OF SUN TO MAKE READY FOR MEETING YOUR ANCESTORS.
TELL HIM I'M IN NO HURRY.

NO COASTWATCHER WOULD BE SO ILL-EQUIPPED AND UNARMED. THIS IS JUST A HARMLESS BEACHCOMBER, BUT HE WILL BE EXECUTED JUST THE SAME, AS A WARNING TO THE NATIVES.

Wally waited—

RICE-CAKES, JAP GROG, EVEN MATCHES AND BACCY FOR ME OLD PIPE! I'D BE ENJOYING THIS IF IT WASN'T FOR HAVING ME HEAD CUT OFF IN THE MORNING.

Night settled.

YOU ARE DISMISSED TO BEACH CAMP. THE CHIEF ORDERS ME TO TAKE OVER GUARD ON FOREIGN DEVIL.

HOLD ON, MATE. I AIN'T SUPPOSED TO GET CHOPPED TILL DAWN.

NO, NO, NOT HARM YOU. YOU SAVE LIFE OF THIS PERSON IN SWAMP.

THIS'LL GET YOU IN TROUBLE, TOJO.

NAME NOT TOJO, BUT SAWADA — GENJA SAWADA. I PAY DEBT OF HONOUR, THEN MUST KILL MYSELF FOR FAILING IN DUTY TO EMPEROR.

NOT SO QUICK, MATE. YOU AIN'T PAID ME BACK TILL I'M SAFE OFF THIS BEACH.

IS TRUE. HONOUR DEBT MUST BE FULLY PAID BEFORE I FREE TO KILL UNWORTHY SELF.

Wally and rescuer stole into the village—
ALL THE PEOPLE, POKO — QUICK AND QUIET. I AIN'T LEAVING ANYBODY TO FACE THEM JAPS.
NOT 'ARF, MATE.

NOTICE HOW GOOD THEY TALK ENGLISH. TAUGHT 'EM MESELF.
AH SO!

Came the dawn—
THE PRISONER AND SEAMAN SAWADA GONE, SIR — THE VILLAGE EMPTY. DO I LEAD OUT A PATROL?
WE CAN SPARE NEITHER MEN NOR TIME. THE RAFT MUST BE COMPLETE AND LOADED BY SUNDOWN SO THAT TOMORROW WE START THE STOWING OF STORES ASHORE.
In the swamp—
MATE, STANDS TO REASON YOU CAN'T BE BOTH RIGHT AND WRONG TO PAY BACK YOUR DEBT TO ME. WHY NOT TAKE A FEW DAYS TO THINK IT OVER?
YOU SPEAK WITH WISDOM. AFTER ALL, IT BE TOO LATE ONCE I KILL MYSELF.
THAT TAKES CARE OF HIM. NOW I'VE GOT TO THINK OF A WAY OF GETTING RID OF THAT JAP SUB.
That night—
SIR, IT IS STRANGE, BUT I SEEM TO SMELL TOBACCO SMOKE.
THE SMOKING LAMP IS LIT. THE BLOWERS MUST BE BRINGING IT UP FROM BELOW.
DIESEL FUEL! BURNS WELL, BUT NEEDS A BIT OF SETTING ALIGHT.
ME OLD PIPE OUGHT TO DO THE TRICK. DUNNO WHAT'S IN THIS JAP BACCY, BUT IT BURNS LIKE OLD ROPE.
CURIOUS! NOW I AM SMELLING BURNING.
SIR — THE RAFT! FIRE!

HOPE I AIN'T DONE TOO MUCH DAMAGE. BE AWKWARD BEING STUCK HERE WITH A WHOLE CREW OF SHIPWRECKED JAPS.

At dawn—
SOME HEAT DAMAGE INCLUDING WARPING OF ATTACK PERISCOPE HOUSING, BUT WE ARE STILL ACTION-WORTHY.
YET MOST OF THE FUEL IS LOST AND THE FIRE MAY HAVE BEEN OBSERVED. I FEAR THIS ISLAND HAS LOST ITS POTENTIAL AS A STRIKE BASE.

And so—
THE IRON CANOE LEAVES.

Wally resumed his castaway life—
YOU'LL JUST HAVE TO GRIT YER TEETH AND TRY TO GET USED TO IT, GENJA.
AH SO! I TRY HARD.

Until—
SEE, MATE! IRON CANOE COME.
CRIPES, IT'S THE OLD TEARAWAY. SHE MUST HAVE COME TO CHECK ON THAT FIRE.

WE GO TO SWAMP!
NO, GENJA, YOU GO TO SWAMP. LOOKS LIKE DUTY'S JUST CAUGHT UP WITH WALLY POTTS.
QUITE PEACEFUL, SIR. NATIVES WAVING TO US. BY JOVE, THERE'S A WHITE MAN AMONG THEM.
SOMETHING RATHER FAMILIAR ABOUT HIM, NUMBER ONE.
AHOY, TEARAWAY! PERMISSION TO COME ABOARD?
WALLY — MATE, YOU COME BACK AFTER WAR.
COUNT ON IT, POKO. I'LL BRING THAT SEWING MACHINE FOR YER MISSUS.
Able Seaman Walter Potts returned to duty—
DID YOU HAVE A BAD TIME, LAD?
'ORRIBLE BAD, CHIEF. IT'D CURL YOUR HAIR IF YOU KNEW HOW I HAD TO ROUGH IT!
THE END

FIGARO

FIGARO LOVES FOOD

I'M IN JAIL AGAIN, FIGARO FANS, BUT I'M JUST ABOUT TO ESCAPE!

OH...ER...SHERIFF! CAN YOU COME IN A MINUTE?
EH? OH, VERY WELL!

WHEN HE OPENS THE DOOR I'LL DIVE OUT THROUGH HIS LEGS!

LIKE THIS!

HA! HA! WHOA, BOY! YOU'RE TOO FAT FOR THAT TRICK!

BACK INTO YOUR CELL!
HUH! I'LL TRY SOMETHING ELSE!

SO... OH, SHERIFF! I'VE LOST A PIECE OF THIS JIGSAW PUZZLE. COME AND HELP ME FIND IT!
JIGSAW PUZZLE

NOT LIKELY! I'VE MORE IMPORTANT THINGS TO DO!
H'MM! I'LL TRY THE SOB STUFF!

BOO-HOO! I WANT TO FINISH MY JIGSAW! BOO-HOO!
ALL RIGHT! ALL RIGHT! I'LL HELP YOU FIND THE PIECE!

CAN'T SEE IT ANYWHERE, FIGARO!
HERE'S WHERE I SNEAK OUT!

IT SEEMS TO BE WORKING!
SO!

A GOOD TRY, FIGARO...BUT NOT GOOD ENOUGH!
THUD!

BACK YOU GO!
HUH! I'LL GET OUT NEXT TIME!

LATER... NEXT TIME THE SHERIFF LOOKS IN HE'LL THINK THE CELL'S EMPTY! WHEN HE COMES IN TO INVESTIGATE, I'LL JUMP ON HIM, THEN ESCAPE!

FIGARO! WHERE'S HE GONE?
JIGSAW PUZZLE

YOU UNDER THAT BED, FIGARO?

WATCH THIS, FIGARO FANS! THE GREAT ESCAPE!

OUCH! HE MOVED!
CRASH!

HE'LL HAVE TO STAY HERE FOR A WEEK, SHERIFF!
WHAT A PITY! HO! HO! HE WAS DUE OUT TOMORROW!

REARGUARD!

A detachment of Cromwell's Roundhead troops was fighting a desperate rearguard action against overwhelming odds at Atherton Moor in Yorkshire, during the English Civil War between King and Parliament in 1643.
HERE COME THE KING'S HORSES AGAIN!
BACK! THE ROUNDHEADS' FIRE IS STILL TOO HOT!
WE HAVE BUT LITTLE POWDER AND SHOT LEFT, CAPTAIN DRUMMOND.
DO YOUR BEST, MEN. GENERAL FAIRFAX CHOSE US AS REARGUARD TO HOLD THE ROYALISTS FROM THIS ROAD UNTIL HIS MAIN FORCES HAVE SAFELY WITHDRAWN TO HULL.

THE ROYALISTS WILL DO FOR YOU ALL WITH THEIR NEXT CHARGE, SIR.
I'M ONLY TOO WELL AWARE OF THAT!
I BE NED JARVEY. THESE BE FRIENDS AND VILLAGERS I MUSTERED TO LEND YOU A HAND.
BRAVE FELLOWS! BUT I'LL NOT SEE YOU ALL SLAUGHTERED BY EARL NEWCASTLE'S HORSE REGIMENT!
FINE HORSEMEN HAVE BEEN TUMBLED BY LONGBOWS MANY TIMES BEFORE NOW!
BOWS AND ARROWS! VILLAGE IDIOTS!
WE DO KEEP UP ARCHERY AS A PASTIME IN THESE PARTS.
WHO ARE THOSE MEN IN FRONT OF THE ENEMY POSITION, EARL NEWCASTLE?
JUST A FEW VILLAGE BUMPKINS.
THE ENEMY FIRE IS SLACKENING! SHORT OF SHOT, NO DOUBT! FORWARD!
EGAD! LONGBOW SHAFTS!
AAAGH!

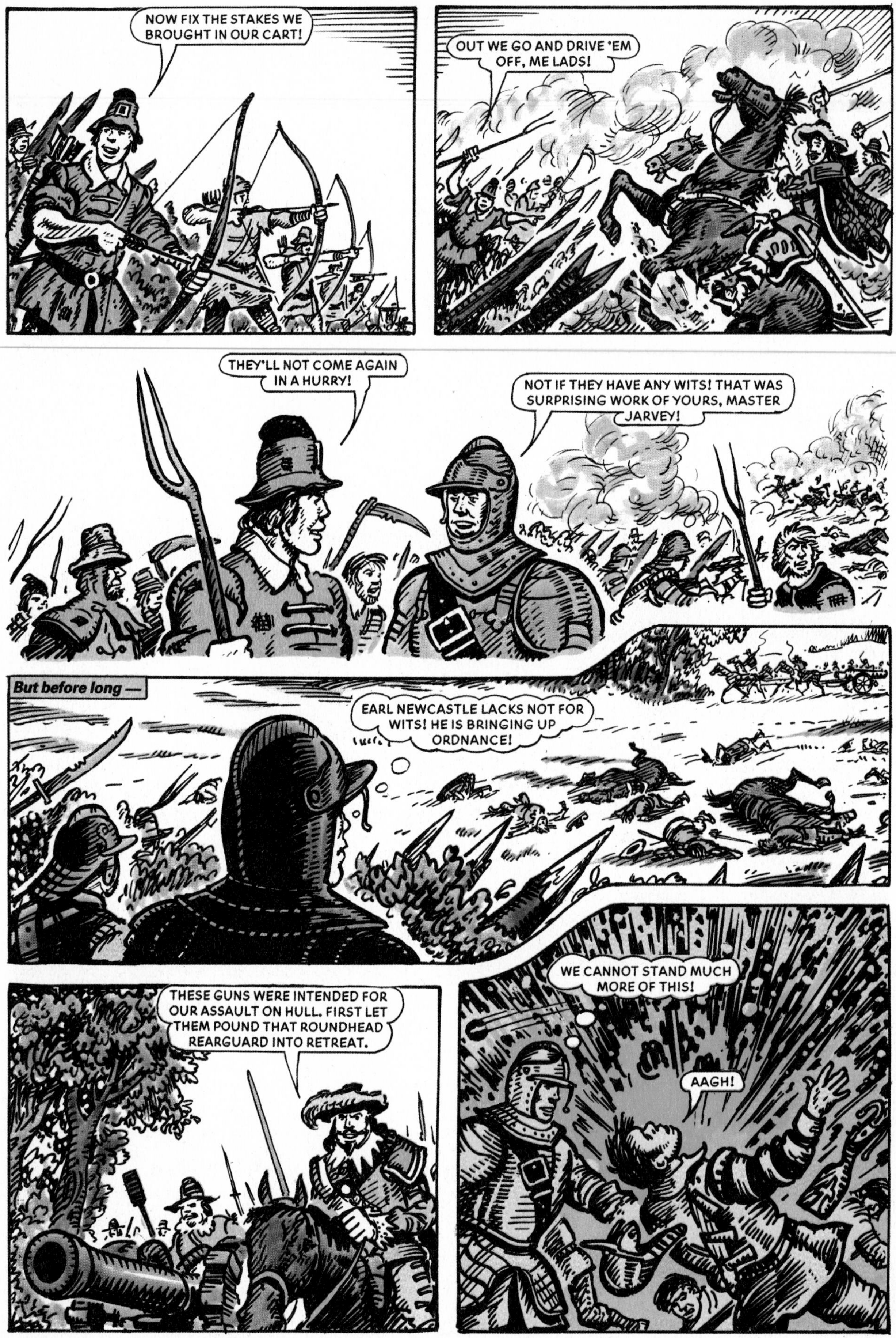

THEY'LL NOT COME AGAIN IN A HURRY!

NOT IF THEY HAVE ANY WITS! THAT WAS SURPRISING WORK OF YOURS, MASTER JARVEY!

But before long —

EARL NEWCASTLE LACKS NOT FOR WITS! HE IS BRINGING UP ORDNANCE!

THESE GUNS WERE INTENDED FOR OUR ASSAULT ON HULL. FIRST LET THEM POUND THAT ROUNDHEAD REARGUARD INTO RETREAT.

WE CANNOT STAND MUCH MORE OF THIS!

AAGH!

WHAT NOW, MASTER JARVEY? YOUR BOWMEN HAVE BROUGHT THIS UPON US BUT THEIR ARROWS CANNOT SILENCE THOSE ENEMY GUNS.
THEN WE'LL NEED TO SILENCE THEM OURSELVES.
USE WHAT POWDER YOU HAVE LEFT TO FIRE THIS HEDGE. 'TIS DRY AS TINDER AND SMOKE WILL BLOW TOWARDS THE ROYALIST GUNS.
Soon—
GET ACROSS THE FIELDS UNDER SCREEN OF THIS SMOKE.
CEASE FIRE UNTIL THAT SMOKE CLEARS.
YOU WOULD BE MOST UNWISE TO USE THAT SWORD, GOOD SIR!
ARMED PEASANTS! RUN!

SPIKING OUR GUNS TO MAKE THEM USELESS!
AYE, SAM TATE OVER THERE IS OUR VILLAGE BLACKSMITH. HE'S RIGHT HANDY AT FORGING IRON SPIKES.
DRIVE THEM OFF! RE-TAKE THE GUNS!
YOU CAN HAVE 'EM NOW! AWAY TO THE WOODS, ME LADS!
After twenty minutes —
WE FEARED THE ROYALIST HORSEMEN HAD CAUGHT YOU.
NOT IN THE WOODS. ALL BOGGY THEY BE AND WE KNOW THE PATHS.
Later, after a messenger had brought the Roundheads orders to retire —
MIND IF WE GO TO HULL WITH YOU, SIR? OUR VILLAGE WAS DESTROYED BY THE ROYALISTS AND WE'VE A MIND TO SERVE YOUR CAUSE.
YOU'VE SERVED IT RIGHT NOBLY ALREADY!
I SHALL COMMEND HIM FOR A COMMISSION, SERGEANT, AND I'LL WAGER THAT WITHIN A YEAR MASTER JARVEY WILL BE AN OUTSTANDING COMMANDER IN OUR IRONSIDE ARMY!
The End

MORGYN the MIGHTY

Morgyn the Mighty, the strongest man in the world, was in the South American country of Venezuela, a desperate appeal from a friend bringing him to the wild forests and jagged peaks of the Sierra del Zamuro.

THIS GORGE ISN'T SHOWN ON WASH'S SKETCH.

MORGYN,
I AM IN PERIL OF MY LIFE. FOLLOW THE ENCLOSED DIRECTIONS AND COME QUICKLY.
Washington Jones

Meanwhile—
NOW WE SHALL SEE IF THE GREAT MORGYN LIVES UP TO HIS REPUTATION.

THE QUICK WAY IS TO CONSTRUCT MY OWN BRIDGE.

EXCELLENT! THIS MORGYN IS IDEAL FOR OUR PURPOSE.

Morgyn came upon the unexpected—

I COULD BELIEVE I WAS IN ROME — ONLY THIS COLISEUM IS BRAND NEW!

A HELICOPTER! THAT'S SOMETHING THE ANCIENT ROMANS NEVER HAD.

At the door of the Coliseum —

MISTER MORGYN — WELCOME! YOUR FRIEND AWAITS YOU.

AN ELEVATOR IS HARDLY WHAT I WOULD EXPECT TO FIND IN THE COLISEUM.

I BUILD SOMEWHAT BETTER THAN THE GREAT VESPASIAN, MY EMPIRE BEING OF MUCH GREATER WEALTH THAN HIS. I AM JUAN VARGAS OF VARGAS OIL.

The elevator descended—
SUDARIO, THIS IS THE GENTLEMAN WHOM WE HAVE BEEN EXPECTING.
SI, PATRON! I LEAD YOU TO WHERE THE SENOR JONES AWAITS.

CAGED BEASTS!
WHAT ELSE WOULD ONE EXPECT UNDER THE COLISEUM, MISTER MORGYN?

SUDARIO FINDS AN ELECTRIC CATTLE-PROD KEEPS THE CREATURES LIVELY.

THAT IS ENOUGH!
AHHH!

DON'T SHOOT, SUDARIO, MISTER MORGYN IS OUR GUEST. SHOW HIM TO HIS FRIEND.

WASH!
MAN, YOU SHOULDN'T HAVE COME. I WOULDN'T HAVE WRITTEN THAT NOTE IF THEY HADN'T FED ME DOPE.

MORGYN, YOU WOULD BE WISE TO RESTRAIN YOUR ANGER AND TAKE NOTE OF THE PENDANT BEING FONDLED BY SUDARIO — AN ELECTRONIC DEVICE THAT DETONATES EXPLOSIVES BY RADIO WAVE.

NOW OBSERVE THE BELT ABOUT THE WAIST OF MISTER JONES — SIX OUNCES OF PLASTIC THAT CAN BE SET OFF BY A FINGER PRESSURE FROM SUDARIO. IT WILL ALSO ACTIVATE AT ANY ATTEMPT TO UNCLASP THE BELT WITHOUT USE OF THE DIAL COMBINATION.

YET THERE IS NO NEED FOR MISTER JONES TO BE EXPLODED — AS LONG AS YOU ACT REASONABLY, MORGYN. YOU WILL START BY JOINING MYSELF AND TWO FRIENDS IN VIEWING A LITTLE ENTERTAINMENT.

They ascended on stairs that moved to the touch of a button—
IN THIS WORLD ARE THOSE WHO CONTROL MORE POWER THAN EVER DREAMED OF BY THE EMPEROR VESPASIAN. LIKE HIM, WE HAVE THE NEED TO RELAX, TO SHED FOR A WHILE THE TERRIBLE BURDEN OF OUR RESPONSIBILITY.

MORGYN, ALLOW ME TO INTRODUCE JAY-JAY HOBB OF TEXAS AND MISTER YU CHI OF HONG KONG.
HI, BUD!
AN HONOUR, MISTER MORGYN.

MORGYN, BE SEATED. I AM ABOUT TO INSTRUCT SUDARIO TO SEND ON THE FIRST PERFORMERS.

A LEOPARD OR PANTHERA PARDUS VERSUS A WOLVERINE OR GULO GULO, THE GLUTTON OF ARCTIC WASTES.

PUTTING THOSE CREATURES TOGETHER DOES NOT MEAN THEY WILL FIGHT.
THESE WILL FIGHT, MORGYN — THANKS TO DRUG TREATMENT AND A LITTLE CALCULATED BRUTALITY.
BEHOLD!

I GOTTA QUARTER OF A MILLION SAYS THE CAT WINS.
WHY NOT A REAL BET, JAY JAY. I WAGER ONE MILLION ON THE GLUTTON.
Mister Yu Chi won—
A NOBLE SPORT, EH, MORGYN? YET WE WOULD IMPROVE ON IT. WE DECIDED ON A BOUT INVOLVING THE ULTIMATE BEAST, MAN HIMSELF, AND WHO BETTER TO REPRESENT MANKIND THAN ITS STRONGEST MEMBER — YOURSELF!
I'LL GIVE YOU NO SPORT OF THAT KIND, VARGAS.
OH YES, YOU WILL, MISTER MORGYN.
ARHHH!
Morgyn fell—
URH — STRAW! CONSIDERATE OF THEM.

A NEW BEAST, EH? WELCOME! I SHALL TAKE SPECIAL CARE OF YOU.
ARGH!

MORGYN! WE'RE IN A BAD MESS, EH, MAN!
NOT GOOD, WASH — BUT WE HAVE ONE ADVANTAGE OVER THE REST OF THE BEASTS. WE CAN THINK.

TUNGSTEN TOUGHENED STEAL AND NO OBVIOUS DOOR — QUITE A CHALLENGE. NOT THAT I CAN TRY ANYTHING WHILE WASH HAS THAT EXPLOSIVE BUCKLED ABOUT HIM.

That evening—
DINNER IS AT THE COFFEE STAGE, SUDARIO. A GOOD TIME FOR THE MAIN EVENT.

Morgyn was aroused—
THE BACK WALL IS OPENING. THAT GLARE IS NOT DAYLIGHT — BESIDES, DUSK MUST HAVE SETTLED BY NOW.

OLE, BEAST! THE ARENA AWAITS.
THE ARENA!

REMEMBER THE IMPERIAL SALUTE OF THE ANCIENT GLADIATORS, MORGYN — WE WHO ARE ABOUT TO DIE SALUTE YOU! YOUR ADVERSARY HAS BEEN MOST CAREFULLY SELECTED.

A KODIAK BIG BROWN, MORGYN — BIGGER, MORE POWERFUL AND SAVAGE EVEN THAN HIS COUSIN THE GRIZZLY.
THE GUY DON'T HAVE A CHANCE. I'VE SEEN A BIG BROWN KEEP COMING AFTER TAKING A SOFTNOSED THIRTY-THIRTY BULLET THROUGH THE HEART.
I LIKE A LONG SHOT. WHAT ODDS DO YOU OFFER?
SUCH RAW BRUTE STRENGTH IS HARD TO MATCH.
LUCKY FOR ME IT KNOWS NOTHING OF LEVERAGE.
SORRY ABOUT THIS, OLD FELLOW. SO VERY SORRY.
Morgyn was forced to kill the bear.
MOST IMPRESSIVE, MORGYN. YOU WILL NOW RETURN TO YOUR CAGE.
TILL MY NEXT BOUT AND THOSE THAT WILL FOLLOW UNTIL I AM KILLED.

Morgyn again was caged—
IT'S KILL OR BE KILLED UNLESS I CAN FIND A WAY OUT.
THE SMELL TELLS ME THAT SUDARIO IS NEAR. NO WILD CREATURE CAN MATCH THAT FOUL REEK!
YOU DARE INSULT ME! I SHALL SHOW YOU WHO IS THE BOSS HERE.
Morgyn moved with startling speed—
FIRST I'LL TAKE CARE OF THIS EXPLOSIVE EXPLODER.
URHHHH!
NOW THE COMBINATION OF THE EXPLOSIVE BELT. HURRY — OR YOUR NECK WILL CRACK LIKE THAT OF THE BEAR.
MERCY — URH! TWO TURNS TO THE LEFT, TWO TO THE RIGHT, THEN REPEAT.
MORGYN, IT WORKS. I GOT THE BELT OPEN, MAN.
PASS IT TO ME, I HAVE USE FOR THAT EXPLOSIVE.
SUDARIO, ANY TRICKS AND I WILL SHOOT YOU WITH YOUR OWN PISTOL.
YOU WON'T GET AWAY WITH THIS!

Shaggy arms intruded—
AAH — THE GORILLA! HELP ME!

SUDARIO HAS DONE A GOOD JOB OF TURNING A GENTLE JUNGLE CREATURE INTO A KILLER!

Morgyn used the explosive belt—
BOOMM

YOU CAN OPEN MY CAGE FROM SUDARIO'S CONTROL BOARD.

Morgyn located the controls—
IT WORKS, MAN! I AM FREE!

SUDARIO, WHAT IS GOING ON? THAT SOUNDED LIKE AN EXPLOSION.
VARGAS.

SENOR VARGAS, THIS IS MORGYN. I AM FREE — AND I HAVE JUST RELEASED YOUR WHOLE MENAGERIE.

THE BEASTS ARE LOOSE!

WASH, I SUGGEST A SPEEDY DEPARTURE BY THE ELEVATOR.
GOOD THINKING, MAN.

The Vargas party broke up—
GENTLEMEN, I KNOW NOT WHAT IS GOING ON, BUT WE WOULD BE WISE TO WITHDRAW.

LOOK!

WE'LL NEVER MAKE IT!

SENOR VARGAS AND HIS FRIENDS DO NOT APPEAR TO BE ENJOYING THEIR LATEST ROUND OF ENTERTAINMENT.
MAN, I AM GETTING THE SAME IMPRESSION!
The End

IT'S A WACKY WORLD!

Wild elephants often rampage through Sumatran villages at night, causing much damage. Now some villagers have found a way of scaring them off — by playing loud rock 'n' roll music! The elephants can't stand it!

American taxi driver Bruce Ploof was furious about all the deep pot-holes he had to drive over on the roads of his home town of Burlington, Vermont, so under cover of darkness he secretly planted evergreen trees in the holes! The city officials took the hint and repaired the roads.

Ten U.S. Army bases in West Germany are guarded by sentries — and geese! The birds give warning of intruders by cackling, and allow the Army to cut down on manpower.

South African doctors discovered that a native's tummy-ache was caused by £800 worth of gold, which they removed from his stomach by an operation. The man's tribe believed swallowing gold cured headaches!

A thief in Somerset made a big mistake when he tried to steal a car. When he opened the door he found two policemen grinning at him! He had failed to notice them in the unmarked car because its windows were frosted up!

When the Sheriff of Clarkesville, Arkansas, and three other officers tried to make an arrest, they found their suspect to be a very slippery customer! He was having a shower when the lawmen called and fled still covered in soap, which prevented them from getting a grip on him!

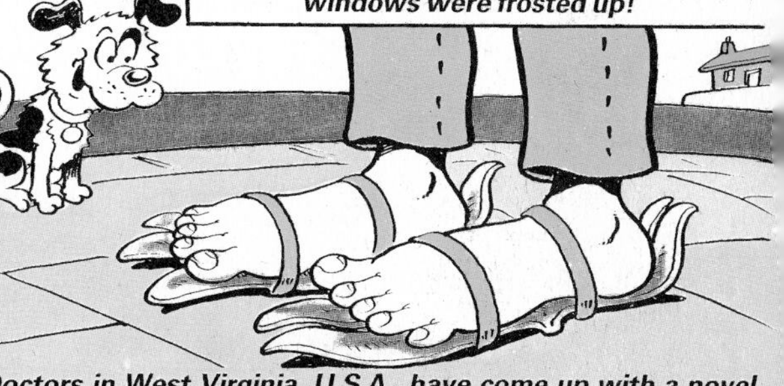

Doctors in West Virginia, U.S.A., have come up with a novel cure for warts. They claim to have cured 150 people by taping banana skins to their feet, mushy side up!

Driving past "The Three Horseshoes" pub near Exeter, Peter Jones was in collision with three runaway horses. Two tried to leap over the car and smashed the windscreen. Peter's face was cut and the car wrecked, but the horses escaped injury. Peter kept a horseshoe in his car for luck!

ANSWERS TO SPORTS CROSSWORD (Page 32)

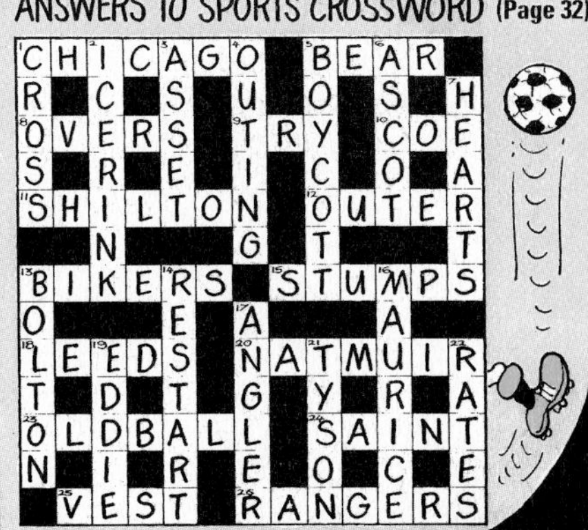

THE CARD TRICK
In World War One a German submarine was shadowing British shipping under destroyer escort in the Atlantic, off the west coast of England—
BRITISH DESTROYER COMING OUR WAY. SHE MAY HAVE SIGHTED OUR PERISCOPE. WE'LL GO DEEPER TILL SHE LOSES INTEREST.
LUCKY FOR US THOSE SURFACE TUBS HAVE NO WAY OF TRACKING US UNDERWATER.
MOTOR WHINE — SCREW WASH. DEFINITELY A SUB, SIR.
SO THIS NEWFANGLED HYDROPHONE GADGET REALLY WORKS.

ADMIRALTY CONFIRMS NONE OF OUR SUBMERSIBLES IS IN THIS AREA. WHICH MEANS WE ARE UP AGAINST A GERMAN U-BOAT.
SUB ALERT, NUMBER ONE. STREAM THE EXPLOSIVE SWEEP.
In the aft motor-room of the U-boat—
THAT'S THE ENGLANDER PASSING OVER. TRUST OLD HANS WHEN HE SAYS THERE'S NOTHING TO WORRY ABOUT.
HANS, I HEAR SOMETHING ELSE . . .
. . . A SORT OF SCRAPING NOISE . . .
HELP! HELP!

WE GOT THE BEGGAR, SIR.
THE SWEEP COULD HAVE SNAGGED ON A REEF OR OLD WRECK. WE'LL TAKE A CLOSER LOOK.

OIL AND DEBRIS, SIR.
FRITZ IS CRAFTY ENOUGH TO DISCHARGE THAT FROM A TORPEDO-TUBE.

NUMBER ONE, WE'RE GOING TO TRY OUT THOSE NEW DEPTH CHARGES.
AYE, AYE, SIR.

The shattered U-boat had settled in twenty fathoms—
BRACE UP, LADS. OLD HANS IS LOOKING AFTER YOU. FIRST WE'LL CHECK ON CONDITIONS FORWARD.

FLOODED! LADS, WE ARE CUT OFF. BRING OUT ALL THE BREATHING SETS.

SEVEN SETS, HANS. THERE ARE EIGHT OF US.
I CAN COUNT, MY BOY. ONE OF US WILL HAVE TO DO WITHOUT. WHAT WILL IT BE — COINS OR CARDS?

Cards were drawn to determine the unlucky crewman—
NOW YOU, HANS. LOW CARD LOSES AND YOU'VE A FOUR TO BEAT.
ONE OF YOU HOLD THIS PACK FOR ME.

HANS, DO YOU BEAT MY FOUR?

I'VE GOT TWO SPOTS — A DEUCE. LOOKS LIKE YOU RASCALS WILL BE LEAVING OLD HANS BEHIND.

Old Hans saw off the escapers —
THAT'S THREE OUT. EASY, ISN'T IT? YOU JUST PADDLE UP THE TWILL-TRUNK AND DRIFT OUT OF THE HATCH.

FIRST TIME I EVER CHEATED AT CARDS, BUT AT LEAST MY LADS HAVE A CHANCE TO LIVE. NOW DO I WAIT TO DROWN OR USE MY LITTLE PISTOL?

ANOTHER EXPLOSION! AREN'T THOSE ENGLANDERS DONE WITH US YET?

More depth-charges exploded round the U-boat —

ACH! SO I DROWN!

WHAT'S THIS?

CARRIED UP IN AN AIR BUBBLE. AM I DREAMING?

A SURVIVOR, SIR!

HE'S UNCONSCIOUS, BUT STILL ALIVE.

Old Hans awoke in the destroyer's sick-bay —
HE SAYS THIS WILL BE SUCH A SURPRISE TO THE LADS HE SENT UP BEFORE HIM.
BREAK IT TO THE POOR FELLOW THAT NO OTHERS CAME UP. THOSE DEPTH-CHARGES MUST HAVE FINISHED THEM.

HE IS THE ONLY ONE WHO SURVIVED.
The End

THE WARS OF HARRY SMITH

Harry Smith, the son of a Cambridgeshire surgeon, joined the local troop of Whittlesey Yeomanry in 1804 when he was sixteen . . . and not too big, as the French prisoners at the Norman Cross Barracks soon pointed out!
I SAY, LEETEL FELLOW, GO HOME TO YOUR MAMMA AND EAT MORE PUDDING!
ONCE ACROSS THE RIVER, WE GO FOR THE BREACH — AND LET NOTHING STOP US. NOTHING I SAY!
The following year, Harry was commissioned into the 2nd Battalion of the 95th Rifles, the famous Greenjackets, and was soon serving in South America — and then with Wellington in the Peninsular War. At the age of 23, he was strong and tough . . . ready to lead a 'forlorn hope' (a body of men picked for hazardous duty) at the storming of Badajoz in 1812.
The French bitterly defended the Spanish fortress with fireballs, burning oil and cannon.
PARDIEU! LET THEM BURN!

The losses were heavy on both sides, but the French were gradually worn down.
SHOW THEM NO MERCY! THEY SHOWED US NONE!
AAAARGH!

After the long siege and hard battle for Badajoz, Wellington allowed his troops two days of looting after the defeat of the enemy.

SEE WHAT I'VE GOT. A FORTUNE IN GEMS!

On the next day Harry and his friend, Johnny Kincaid, were about to enter the town, when . . .

THE DEVIL TAKE IT! I SAID THEY WERE GOING TOO FAR WITH THEIR LOOTING AND RIOTING.

HELP! HELP US!

HALT THERE. THIS IS AS FAR AS YOU GO. THE GENERAL LET YOU TAKE THE BIT BETWEEN YOUR TEETH AFTER THE WAY YOU FOUGHT THE FROGS, BUT ENOUGH IS ENOUGH. BACK WITH YOU!

One of the ladies said she was the wife of a Spanish officer serving elsewhere.

AND THIS IS MY YOUNG SISTER, JUANA MARIA DE LOS DOLORES DE LEON. SEE, THEY TORE OUR EAR-RINGS OUT LIKE BRUTES! WE WERE IN GREAT FEAR!

THEN TAKE COURAGE, MADAM. YOU ARE NOW UNDER OUR CARE AND PROTECTION.

Shortly afterwards, Harry Smith married young Juana at a simple camp ceremony, and thereafter she travelled with him through the Peninsula, though refusing to be a burden to him.

JUANA, I HAVE NOT SEEN YOU ALL DAY. ARE YOU STILL ALL RIGHT?

SI, SI! I AM WELL. GO BACK TO YOUR DUTIES, MY HENRIQUE. I CAN TAKE CARE OF MYSELF.

When the Peninsular War ended in 1814, Harry, then a Brigade-Major, was one of 7,000 of Wellington's veterans sent out to fight in the war with America, and he rode with General Ross at the Battle of Bladensburg, outside Washington.
CLEAR THEM OUT OF IT, HARRY! THEN WASHINGTON WILL BE OURS!
But Harry was not pleased when they burned down the Palace (later known as the White House) and other parliamentary buildings.
GENERAL, I WILL BE HONEST WITH YOU. IT HORRIFIES ME TO SEE SUCH WANTON DESTRUCTION OF FINE BUILDINGS.
'TWAS THE ORDER OF THE GOVERNMENT, HARRY.
THAT'S THE BEST NEWS I COULD HAVE HEARD! I THOUGHT MY FIGHTING DAYS WOULD BE OVER, BUT NOW I STAND A CHANCE OF MAKING LIEUTENANT-COLONEL, WITH BONEY STILL SPOILING FOR BATTLE!

And so Washington fell, the British officers eating a fine banquet in the President's Palace, which President Madison had had prepared for his own 'victorious' officers.

EGAD, I HAVEN'T EATEN SO WELL AS THIS SINCE WE TOOK VITTORIA AND CAPTURED KING JOSEPH'S COACH AND WAGONS!

He came back to England in 1815 in the sloop-of-war 'Brazen'. And as they neared Portsmouth . . .

ARE YOU JUST OUT OF PORTSMOUTH? WHAT IS THE NEWS FROM HOME?

NEWS? THERE IS PLENTY. BONAPARTE IS BACK ON THE THRONE OF FRANCE AGAIN!

Harry fought at Waterloo and survived it, being awarded the C.B. In the years that followed he rose in rank and importance, serving in Scotland, Ireland, the West Indies and Africa. Then in 1843 he served under General Sir Hugh Gough in the Gwalior campaign in India.
DO YOU THINK IT IS SAFE, SIR, FOR OUR LADIES TO BE AT THE HEAD OF THE COLUMN? SUPPOSE WE ARE ATTACKED?
TRY TELLING THAT TO LADY GOUGH, HARRY. SHE REFUSES TO TRAVEL IN THE DUST AT THE REAR. YOUR JUANA WOULD NOT LIKE IT, EITHER.
But the Gwalior rebels were waiting . . .
FIRE!
AIEEEE!
GET THEM TO THE REAR! CANNON-BALLS ARE DEADLIER THAN DUST CLOUDS!
So began the Battle of Maharajpoor, in which the rebels lost all their fifty-four guns. A medal, the Maharajpoor Star, was awarded to those taking part. And when Juana did not receive one, Harry had one made for her in London of precious metals.

EUGH!
THE COLOURS! RALLY ROUND THE COLOURS!
Harry was also awarded the KCB, becoming Major-General Sir Harry Smith, and was commanding a division at the Battle of Moodkee in the First Sikh War of 1845. But he was still a fighting man . . .

Riding his black Arab steed, he snatched up the colours of the 50th Foot . . .
NOW, MEN, FOLLOW ME. ATTACK IS THE BEST DEFENCE!

HERE ARE YOUR COLOURS. NOW COME AND SAVE THEM!

His division overwhelmed the Sikhs, capturing seventeen guns in the action.

AARGH!

UP THE 50TH!

After India, he was appointed Governor of Cape Town in South Africa, and so popular was he there that two new towns in Natal were named after him and his wife. One was Harrismith — but the other became famous in the Boer War of 1900 when it was besieged by the Boers. The town was Ladysmith, named after the young girl Harry had saved at Badajoz in Spain so many years before.

PHOTO

△ 1. These two football captains, who faced each other in the 1966 World Cup Final, are seen here in a "replay" in 1985 in aid of the Bradford Fire Disaster. Who are they?

△ 2. What kind of bird is this and for what purpose is it used by the R.A.F.?

△ 3. This strange-looking aeroplane flew round the world non-stop without refuelling in 1986. What was its name?

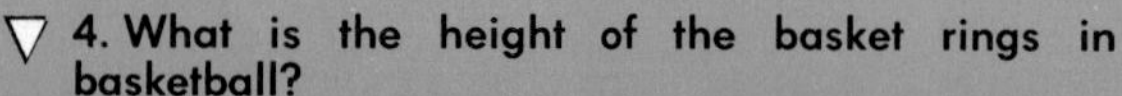

▽ 4. What is the height of the basket rings in basketball?

▽ 5. What is the name of this snake-eating bird of prey?

△ 6. A famous ship is shown being transported back to Dundee, the port where she was built. Can you name the three-masted vessel and the explorer with whom she was connected?

△ 7. What kind of sea creature is this youngster showing off?

QUIZ

△ 8. Which famous stadium is this and in what year did it first open?

9. What is the name of this U.S. Air Force high-flying, intelligence-gathering jet plane? ▽

10. Here are two famous sportsmen wearing unusual gear for them. Who are they? ▽

ANSWERS

1. Bobby Moore of England (left) and Uwe Seeler of West Germany. 2. A peregrine falcon, used for scaring birds away from runways. 3. Voyager. 4. The basket rings are 3.05 metres above the floor. 5. The secretary bird. 6. Captain Scott's "Discovery". 7. A squid. 8. Wembley Stadium opened in 1923. 9. Blackbird. 10. England footballer Glenn Hoddle and snooker's Tony Knowles (inset).

FIGARO

I'LL ROB THE NEXT PERSON WHO COMES ALONG THE TRAIL!

HERE'S SOMEONE NOW!

I'M IN LUCK! IT'S HIRAM J. VANDERBULB! HE'S A MILLIONAIRE!

I WON'T DETAIN YOU, SIR! JUST HAND OVER YOUR WALLET!
MM? OH, VERY WELL!

DEAR ME! IT'S GONE! MUST HAVE BOUNCED OUT ON THIS BUMPY ROAD!
!

I DON'T LIKE HARD WORK, BUT THAT WALLET'S BOUND TO BE LOADED WITH CASH!

I'LL FIND YOUR WALLET, MR VANDERBULB!
MM? NO NEED TO, REALLY!

IT MIGHT BE AMONG THAT PRICKLY CACTUS!
YES, IT MIGHT!

OW!
OH!
AAH!
OOH!

NO!...GASP....IT ISN'T THERE!
PITY!

L-LOOK!
OH, YES! THAT'S IT!

AT LAST! AT LAST!
RUMBLE!

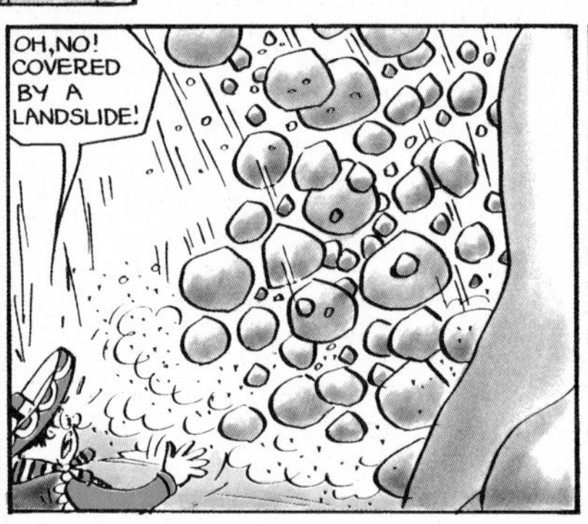
OH, NO! COVERED BY A LANDSLIDE!

MUST GET IT! I MUST!
IT'S NOT WORTH ALL THE BOTHER, REALLY!

GASP! I-I GOT IT!

NOW! LET'S SEE HOW MUCH MONEY I CAN PINCH FROM IT!
EH? MONEY?

TH-THERE'S NO MONEY IN IT!
OF COURSE NOT...

...I NEVER CARRY ANY MONEY OUT ON THE PRAIRIE. TOO MANY OF YOU BANDIT CHAPPIES ABOUT!

The Old School Tie

Waverley School put its stamp on a multitude of boys since being founded by Royal Charter in the reign of Elizabeth the First. Many gained a fame that earned them an inscription on the walls of Great Hall, but the supreme distinction for any old boy was for his name to be recorded in the Rotunda — the Waverley Hall of Fame.

MY VISITS BACK HERE DO ME A POWER OF GOOD, HEADMASTER. REMEMBERING THE DOINGS OF SOME OF THE OLD BOYS KNOCKS THE SWANK OUT OF ME.

GENERAL HAYWARD, I AM SURE YOUR MILITARY RECORD ENTITLES YOU TO A CERTAIN, ER, SWANK.

I HEAR YOUR SON HAS FOLLOWED YOU INTO THE SERVICE.
TOM DID START IN THE REGIMENT, HEADMASTER, BUT NOW HE'S IN ONE OF THESE SPECIAL SERVICE CROWDS. AT PRESENT HE'S ON AN ARCTIC EXERCISE.

In the Arctic —
THAT'S THE CHARGE SET! NOW TO GET OUT OF HERE!
THERE SHE BLOWS — ON THE DOT.
JOB NICELY WRAPPED UP, SKIPPER. NOW YOU CAN SWAN OFF MERRILY TO YOUR NEW POSTING IN THE SUNSHINE.
MILITARY ADVISER, EH? I THOUGHT ONLY ELDERLY BUFFERS WERE PICKED FOR THAT KIND OF JOB.
USUALLY, JOE, BUT IT SEEMS THIS PARTICULAR STATE IN THE UNITED ARAB EMIRATES FAVOURS FELLOWS FROM WAVERLEY SCHOOL.

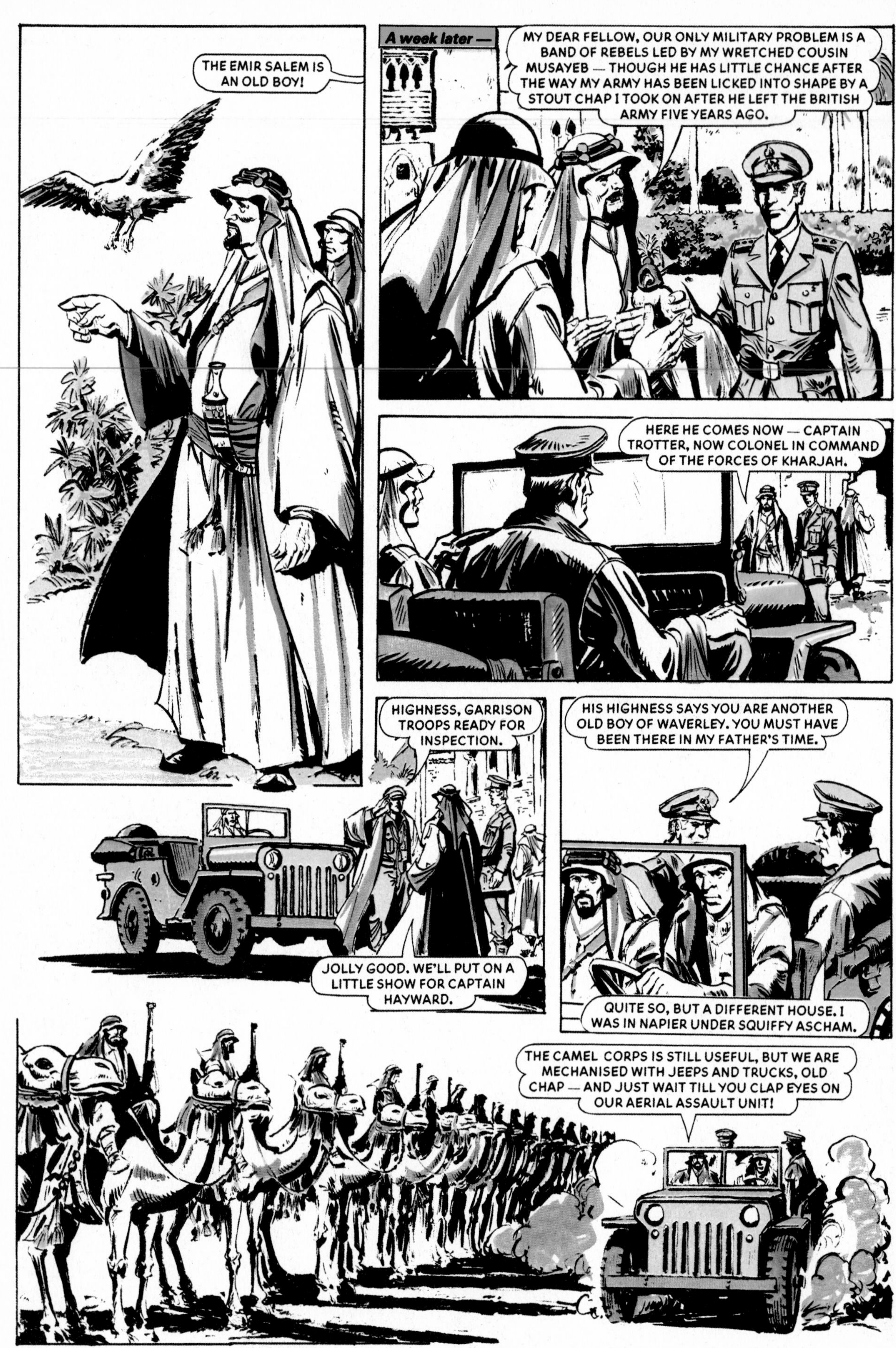
THE EMIR SALEM IS AN OLD BOY!
A week later —
MY DEAR FELLOW, OUR ONLY MILITARY PROBLEM IS A BAND OF REBELS LED BY MY WRETCHED COUSIN MUSAYEB — THOUGH HE HAS LITTLE CHANCE AFTER THE WAY MY ARMY HAS BEEN LICKED INTO SHAPE BY A STOUT CHAP I TOOK ON AFTER HE LEFT THE BRITISH ARMY FIVE YEARS AGO.
HERE HE COMES NOW — CAPTAIN TROTTER, NOW COLONEL IN COMMAND OF THE FORCES OF KHARJAH.
HIGHNESS, GARRISON TROOPS READY FOR INSPECTION.
JOLLY GOOD. WE'LL PUT ON A LITTLE SHOW FOR CAPTAIN HAYWARD.
HIS HIGHNESS SAYS YOU ARE ANOTHER OLD BOY OF WAVERLEY. YOU MUST HAVE BEEN THERE IN MY FATHER'S TIME.
QUITE SO, BUT A DIFFERENT HOUSE. I WAS IN NAPIER UNDER SQUIFFY ASCHAM.
THE CAMEL CORPS IS STILL USEFUL, BUT WE ARE MECHANISED WITH JEEPS AND TRUCKS, OLD CHAP — AND JUST WAIT TILL YOU CLAP EYES ON OUR AERIAL ASSAULT UNIT!

HELICOPTERS FOR WHIZZING OUR CHAPS INTO ACTION AND SUPPLYING OUTPOSTS. THE LITTLE SCOUT MACHINE IS MY FAVOURITE. WE'LL GO FOR A LITTLE FLIGHT.

HIGHNESS, I HAVE TO SAY AGAIN THIS ISN'T WISE. IT MEANS YOUR BODYGUARD HAS TO BE LEFT BEHIND.
TROTTER, STOP BEING SUCH AN OLD FUDDY-DUDDY. I REALLY THINK YOU JUST DISTRUST MY FLYING.

NIFTY TAKE-OFF, EH, HAYWARD? MY INSTRUCTOR ASSURES ME I AM QUITE READY TO TAKE MY PILOT'S LICENCE.
ER — THAT'S A COMFORT, HIGHNESS.

SIR, I WAS LONG AFTER YOUR TIME AT WAVERLEY, BUT THE NAME OF TROTTER SEEMS TO RING A BELL.
MUST HAVE BEEN SOME OTHER TROTTER, OLD CHAP. SHALL I FILL YOU IN ON MY OUTPOST SYSTEM FOR PENNING IN THE REBELS?

THE LAVA BENDS, HAYWARD — THE LAIR OF COUSIN MUSAYEB'S GANG. AWKWARD TERRAIN FROM WHICH TO WINKLE THEM OUT.

HIGHNESS, YOU ARE FLYING TOO LOW.
DASH IT, TROTTER, I'M TRYING TO GIVE HAYWARD A GOOD VIEW.

VAPOUR TRAIL — A MISSILE! EVADE, HIGHNESS — EVADE!

MISSILE EVADING WAS NOT INCLUDED IN MY INSTRUCTION.
YOU'RE DOING GREAT, HIGHNESS. LET'S HOPE THE BIRD ISN'T A HEAT-SEEKER.

PHEW! THAT WAS CLOSE!

The missile exploded close to the helicopter.

WE SEEM TO HAVE SUFFERED DAMAGE — I HAVE NO CONTROL.
KEEP TRYING, HIGHNESS. YOUNG HAYWARD AND I WILL KEEP OUR FINGERS CROSSED.

SUCH A PITY MY INSTRUCTOR IS NOT HERE TO ADVISE.

WELL, WE'RE DOWN!
HAYWARD, TAKE CARE OF HIS HIGHNESS WHILE I TRY FOR A MAYDAY.
RIGHT, SIR, BUT DON'T BE TOO LONG. THERE'S A NASTY SMELL OF SPILLED FUEL.

THEY DO SAY ANY LANDING IS GOOD IF ONE CAN WALK AWAY FROM IT.
MIGHT BE BETTER IF WE WALKED QUICKLY FROM THIS ONE, SIR.
DIDN'T GET AN ANSWER, BUT RECEPTION COULD BE SCREENED IN THIS LAVA. WE'LL JUST HAVE TO HOPE SOMEBODY HEARD ME!
AT LEAST YOU SALVAGED WATER AND A MEDICAL BAG. GOOD THINKING, SIR.
JUST AS WELL IT HASN'T BREWED OR THOSE REBELS WOULD HAVE A HOMING BEACON.
HAYWARD, MY GUESS IS THOSE RASCALS KNOW EXACTLY WHERE WE ARE. WHAT I'M WONDERING IS HOW THEY GOT HOLD OF THAT MISSILE-LAUNCHER.
ARGH! MY LEG! I'VE BEEN SHOT!
THE BULLET GOT HIM IN THE LOWER LEG.
LET'S MOVE HIM INTO COVER. WE'RE SITTING DUCKS OUT HERE.
I'LL COVER YOU!

A RIFLE AND A PISTOL ISN'T MUCH FIRE-POWER TO STAND OFF A RUSH.
THAT'S NOT THEIR STYLE, LAD. BY DAY THEY'LL JUST SNIPE US. IT'S AT NIGHT WHEN WE'LL BE DONE FOR IF WE'RE NOT OUT OF HERE!

THAT'S WHEN THEY'LL SLIP IN WITH THEIR KNIVES!

The day slowly passed.
I WAS HOPING THAT AMERICAN RIG HAD PICKED UP MY SIGNAL EVEN IF THE BARRACK OPERATOR WAS TAKING A TEA-BREAK —
HUSH — LISTEN!

LOOK!

WE ARE SAVED.

SOMETHING'S GOING ON OVER YONDER. BY GOLLY, IT'S A LAUNCHER — AN OLD REDEYE GROUND TO AIR JOB!

THOSE CHOPPERS ARE GOING TO BE POTTED LIKE GROUSE.
FOUR HUNDRED YARDS IS LONG RANGE FOR A RIFLE. ANYWAY, THEY'D ONLY SHIFT INTO COVER IF I OPENED UP. SO THERE'S ONLY ONE WAY.
Trotter fired!
THAT'LL GIVE ME SOME COVER. TAKE MY PISTOL AND WATCH OVER HIS HIGHNESS.
Trotter moved.
WHERE IS HE?
HARD TO SEE IN THE SMOKE — AH! THERE HE GOES. THAT OLD BUFFER CAN MOVE.
AAAH!
NOW FOR THE OTHER TWO!

I DID IT, B'GAD, BUT I'M DONE FOR! COME ON IN, LADS — DO A GOOD JOB OF MOPPING UP.

INSHALLAH!

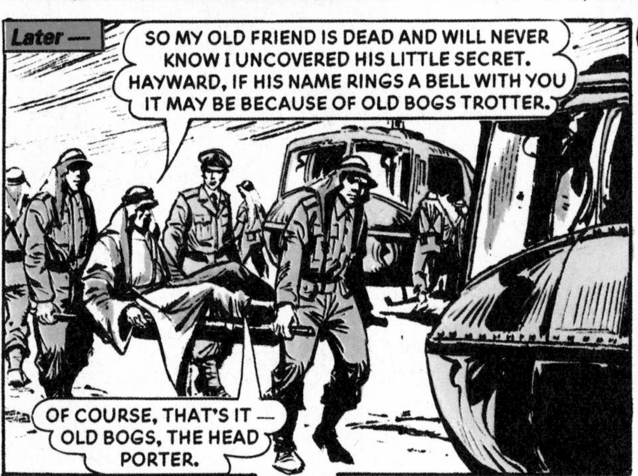
Later —
SO MY OLD FRIEND IS DEAD AND WILL NEVER KNOW I UNCOVERED HIS LITTLE SECRET. HAYWARD, IF HIS NAME RINGS A BELL WITH YOU IT MAY BE BECAUSE OF OLD BOGS TROTTER.
OF COURSE, THAT'S IT — OLD BOGS, THE HEAD PORTER.

TROTTER WAS THE SON OF OLD BOGS. HE WAS ONLY EVER AT WAVERLEY AS A BOOT BOY AND HE GAINED HIS COMMISSION THE HARD WAY THROUGH THE RANKS. HE LIED TO GET THIS POSITION WITH ME — AND PERHAPS BECAUSE OF A GENUINE FEELING FOR THE OLD SCHOOL.

Waverley School, six months later, and General Hayward was about to perform an important task.
I AM HONOURED TO UNVEIL HERE IN OUR OWN HALL OF FAME A TRIBUTE TO A MAN WHOM OUR SCHOOL IS PROUD TO REGARD AS ONE OF ITS OWN.

GEORGE TROTTER
THE END

The HAMMER MAN

Seeking their fortunes as bounty hunters for rewards in the days of King Henry the Fifth, former blacksmith Baron Chell Puddock and Sir Jack Jinks happened to be spectators at a jousting tournament, where they witnessed a dreadful crime.

GADZOOKS! YONDER KNIGHT HAS STOLEN THE GRAND GOLD MELEE TROPHY, LORD CHELL!

FOUL FELONY!

WHAT KNIGHT WOULD DO SO DASTARDLY A DEED?
MAY WE OFFER OUR SERVICES, LORD LESTER?

FORTY CROWNS REWARD FOR RETURN OF THE TROPHY!
GOODLY PAY! TO HORSE AND AWAY!

DID YOU PERCEIVE A KNIGHT IN HASTY FLIGHT?
AYE! NEAR RODE US DOWN! HE WENT THAT WAY OUT OF TOWN!

Soon, in nearby woods—
THERE GOES THE MISCREANT!
I'LL KNOCK HIS NOGGIN!

WELL THROWN!

GADZUMPS! I'VE KNOCKED HIS PATE CLEAN OFF!

But then—
A FAIR DAMSEL!
COMPLETE WITH HER NOGGIN!

A HELM TOO BIG FOR HER PRETTY PATE!
LIKEWISE THIS SUIT OF MAIL! PRAY EXPLAIN, FAIR MAID!

HERE'S THE GOLD TROPHY PRIZE!
I MEANT NOT TO STEAL BUT ONLY TO BORROW IT FOR A WHILE.

I AM LADY CLAUDIA. MY FATHER, SIR PERCY PUMFRET, LIES SORELY SICK AT OUR CASTLE. HE HELD THAT TROPHY AS CHAMPION FOR SO MANY YEARS THAT HE WAS EVENTUALLY GIVEN IT TO KEEP. BUT WE HAD TO SELL IT WITH OTHER VALUABLES TO AID OUR VILLAGERS WHEN THEY FELL UPON HARD TIMES.

NOW IN HIS SICKNESS MY POOR FATHER FORGETS WE SOLD THE TROPHY BACK TO THE TOURNEY MARSHAL. HE KEEPS CALLING FOR IT AS IF IT MAY RESTORE THE HEALTH OF HIS YOUNGER DAYS. HENCE, I GUISED MYSELF IN SOME ARMOUR AND SET OUT TO PURLOIN IT FROM THE TOURNEY.
A SAD TALE, FORSOOTH.

Suddenly—
WE'LL TAKE THAT, SIR HAMMERHEAD!

ROBBERS!
NAY! THE SWYPER BROTHERS, BOUNTY HUNTERS LIKE OURSELVES. THEY MUST HAVE FOLLOWED US FROM THE TOURNEY.

ODDS GRIPES! THE KNAVES RIDE FAST STEEDS. THEY'LL SOON BE BACK AT THE TOURNEY TO CLAIM THAT FORTY CROWNS REWARD.
NO HOPE NOW OF MY POOR FATHER REGAINING HIS HEALTH!
WEEP NOT, FAIR MAID. I HAVE A PLAN.

At Sir Percy's nearby castle—
THUS WEARING YOUR FATHER'S JOUSTING MAIL I SHALL ENTER THE TOURNEY GUISED AS SIR PERCY'S ACCREDITED CHAMPION!
AND THUS REGAIN THE TROPHY FOR US? HOW GALLANT!

METHINKS YOUR GALLANTRY EXCEEDS YOUR WISDOM!
PERCHANCE SO, LORD CHELL. GLADLY WOULD I HAVE LEFT THIS AFFRAY TO YOU, BUT SIR PERCY'S ARMOUR MIGHT NOT FIT YOU SO WELL.

At the tourney, where the Gold Trophy had been returned—
SIR PERCY PUMFRET'S CHAMPION TO JOIN IN THE GRAND MELEE! LAST KNIGHT LEFT ON HIS FEET TO WIN THE GRAND GOLD TROPHY!

GADSWOES! I DARE NOT LOOK!
AAAH!
CRASH!
CLANG!

I CAN STAND ASIDE NO MORE FROM THIS MERRY WAR!
SIR PERCY'S CHAMPION IS HARD PRESSED!

WHAM!
YAROOOF!
BARON CHELL ENTERS THE AFFRAY LATE IN THE DAY!

Later, back at Sir Percy's castle—
YOURS NOW TO KEEP!
MY HERO! MY CHAMPION!
RESTORING SIR PERCY'S HEALTH HAS DONE NAUGHT TO RESTORE OUR WEALTH!
THIS SCARF AS TOKEN OF A FAIR DAMSEL'S FAVOUR IS ALL THE WEALTH A TRUE KNIGHT DESIRES.
Next day—
LET US HOPE YONDER KENTISH TOWN OFFERS US MORE PROFITABLE EMPLOY.
OYEZ! OYEZ! YE MAYOR OFFERS A HUNDRED CROWNS REWARD FOR SLAYING OF YE DREADFUL DRAGON.
WHAT DOLTISH DRIVEL IS THIS?
'TIS NO DRIVEL! A DREAD DRAGON HAS COME TO LURK ON NEARBY DIMWIT DOWNS. SAVE US, NOBLE KNIGHTS!
HOORAY!
ODDS CHEERS! A HUNDRED CROWNS FOR FREEING FOLKS FROM FOOLISH FEARS!

Soon—
YONDER IS THE CAVE SAID TO BE THE DRAGON'S LAIR.
DOUBTLESS THE SORT OF MOCK DRAGON WE HAVE OFT MET ELSEWHERE.

A CONTRAPION OF PAINTED WOOD WITH KNAVES LURKING INSIDE!
ONE MERRY TAP WILL CRACK ITS HIDE!

OOAAAH!
BLANNG!
MY SWORD SNAPS!

GROOAARR!
YEEAOW!

GADSTEETH! CAN IT BE A TRUE DRAGON AFTER ALL?
NAY, 'TIS MADE OF IRON. SEE HOW IT BROKE MY SWORD AND NEAR SHIVERED YOUR HAMMER.

WE ARE NEAR A COAST OFT PLAGUED BY FRENCH RAIDERS. MAYHAP THIS DRAGON IS SOME FIENDISH DEVICE BROUGHT ASHORE BY THE FRENCH TO AFFRIGHT LOCAL FOLKS AND THUS AID A COMING RAID.

So, that night—
'TIS TO BE WONDERED WHY THE TOWN MILITIA DID NOT THINK TO USE SUCH KEGS OF GUNPOWDER TO ASSAIL THE DRAGON.
NONE IS BRAVE ENOUGH EVEN TO APPROACH ITS LAIR.

WELCOME TO MERRIE ENGLAND, FRENCHY KNAVES!

KERBOOOM!
EEAAGH!

YIELD, FROGGIES!
GADSWOE! WE ARE NO FRENCHIES BUT SKILLED ARMOURERS AND CRAFTSMEN FROM KING HENRY'S ROYAL ORDNANCE WORKS!

Inside the cave—
I AM MASTER CRAFTSMAN WATTS, ENTRUSTED TO PERFECT THIS WONDROUS NEW WEAPON OF WAR.
AN IRON DRAGON ON CONCEALED BOMBARD WHEELS!

'TIS DRIVEN BY STEAM POWER FROM THIS BOILER. SMITHY BELLOWS GUSH OUT SMOKE AND FIRE TO AFFRIGHT THE FOE.
A FEARSOME DEVICE! BUT WHY ALSO AFFRIGHT THE LOCAL FOLKS?

MERELY TO KEEP THEM FROM PRYING TOO CLOSELY INTO OUR SECRET WORKS.
THE TOWN BELLS RING ALARM! FRENCH RAIDERS HAVE LANDED!

JUST THE CHANCE WE AWAITED TO TEST OUT OUR WAR DRAGON! NOW YOU HAVE DONE IT AND MY MEN TOO MUCH MISCHIEF TO SAVE THE TOWN FROM ENEMY ASSAULT!
SHOW US HOW AND WE WILL MAN THE DREAD DEVICE!

So, soon—
ONCE IN MOTION THE DRAGON WILL ROLL DOWN TOWARDS THE TOWN. LET US PRAY THE FRENCH MAY THEN TURN AND FLEE!

PHEW! 'TIS HOT! BACK TO MY BLACKSMITH'S BRAZIER AND BELLOWS!
'TIS NOT EASY TO STEER STRAIGHT.

WE MOVE AT SPEED! HOW DO WE STOP?
ALAS, WE FORGOT TO ASK!

LOOT AND BURN!
SACRE BLEU! LOOK WHAT COMES!

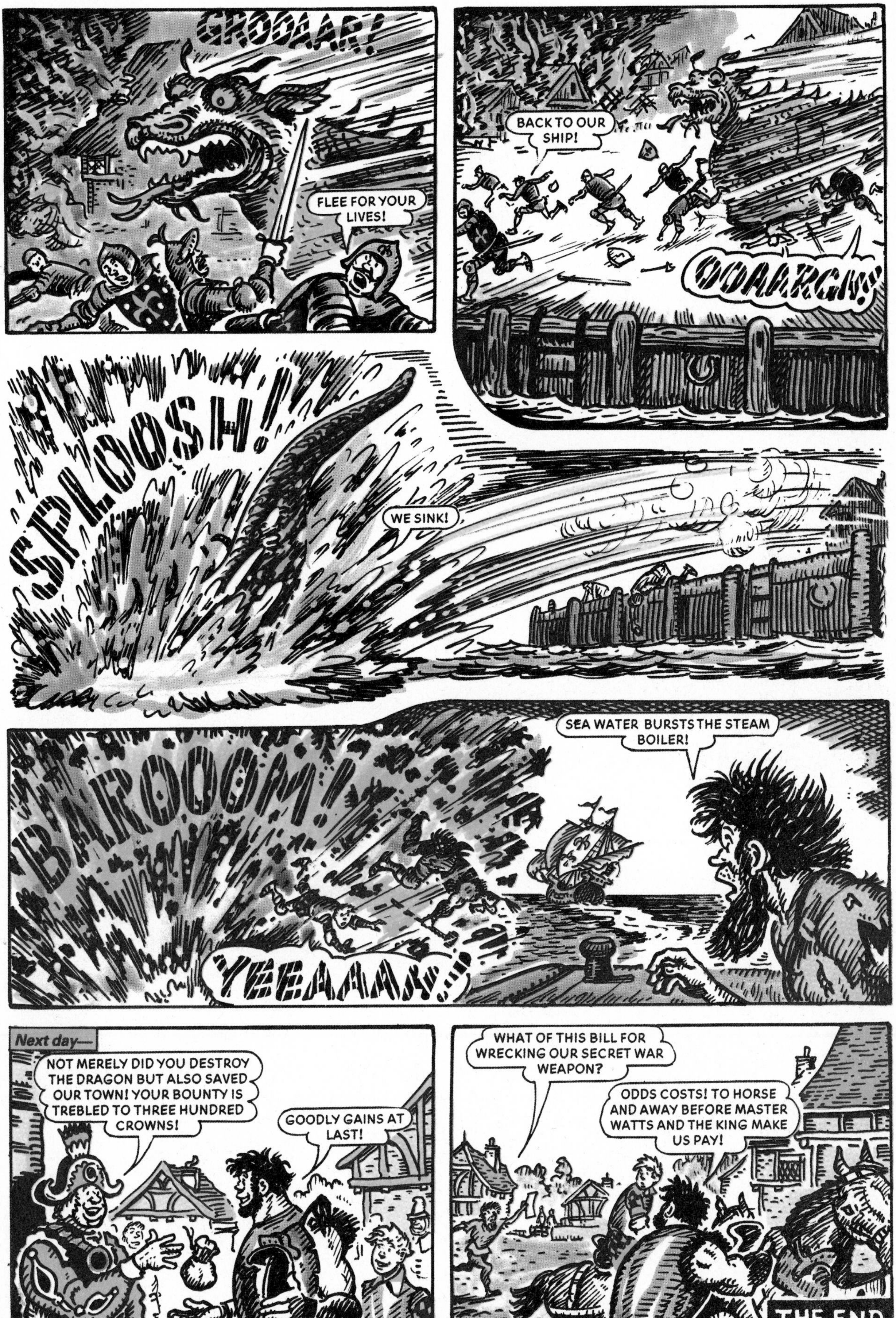

GROOAAR!

FLEE FOR YOUR LIVES!

BACK TO OUR SHIP!

OOARRGH!

SPLOOSH!!

WE SINK!

SEA WATER BURSTS THE STEAM BOILER!

BAROOOM!!

YEEAAAH!!!

FIGARO

HUSH, READERS! FIGARO IS IN BED!

BUT I'M NOT ASLEEP. THE GANG ARE ON HOLIDAY AND IT'S VERY LONELY HERE!

IN FACT, IF I WEREN'T SO BRAVE I-I'D BE SCARED!

ULP! A NOISE!
RUSTLE!

OOH! A B-BURGLAR!

H-HAVE PITY ON A P-POOR MAN! THERE'S N-NOTHING WORTH PINCHING HERE!
YOU'RE RIGHT!

WHAT A LOAD OF OLD RUBBISH!
HA! I SURE SCARED HIM OFF!

NEXT MORNING...
I'M OFF TO BUY SOME EXTRA GUNS IN CASE MY SHACK'S BURGLED AGAIN!

BUT WHILE FIGARO'S AWAY...
THAT SHACK'S RIGHT IN THE PATH OF THE NEW RAILROAD! WE'LL GET THE OWNER TO SHIFT IT!

NOBODY IN! WELL, WE CAN'T WASTE TIME... WE'LL HAVE TO MOVE IT!
PLAN

I'M WELL ARMED NOW!
BULLETS

M-MY SHACK! THOSE CHEEKY BURGLARS ARE PINCHING THE WHOLE THING!

PUT MY SHACK BACK, YOU ROBBERS —OR ELSE!
YOU DON'T UNDERSTAND, SIR!

PUT IT BACK OR I SHOOT!
VERY WELL... BUT YOU'LL BE SORRY!
PLAN

NEXT NIGHT...
AH, WELL—AT LEAST I'M NOT LONELY TONIGHT!

THE GREAT CONKER BATTLE

Kitchener Road Junior School, in the days before the Second World War, was the scene of the Great Conker Battle.

FIFTY MARBLES — AND I'M OFFERING TWO TO ONE ON ANY OF YER READY TO TAKE ON ME CHAMPION CONKER-THIRTY.
I'LL TAKE YER, SPIKE. I'LL EVEN LET THAT BEAT-UP OLD CONK TAKE FIRST SWIPE AT ME BRAN' NEW CONTENDER.

TELL YER WHAT — HOW ABOUT STAKING ALL OUR MARBLES ON THIS ONE SWIPE?
THAT'S FINE BY ME IF YER REALLY WANTS TO GIVE 'EM AWAY, TED HICKS.

AHH — CRIPES!

THERE GOES TED WITH YER WINNINGS FOR THE WHOLE CONKER SEASON.
AW, HIS ROOKIE CONKER WAS JUST LUCKY. THERE'S NEVER BEEN A CHAMP THAT NOTCHED UP A SCORE OF THIRTY KILLS LIKE THIS 'UN DID!

Years later, caught up in the retreat to Dunkirk, a Royal Artillery field battery found its way across a road junction blocked by German self-propelled guns.

OFF THE ROAD! CRASH ACTION!

SIR, I'VE JUST HAD WORDS WITH A SERGEANT LEADING A BUNCH OF INFANTRY STRAGGLERS. HE HAD TO SLIP PAST JERRY AND CAN GIVE US A MAP REFERENCE ON THE GUNS.

WE NEED MORE ACCURACY THAN A PREDICTED SHOOT. ASK THE CHAP IF HE'LL GUIDE A SPOTTING PARTY.

Gunner-Signaller Spike Watts met an old schoolmate.

TED HICKS! LUMME, HOW'D YOU MANAGE TO WANGLE THREE TAPES?

WON 'EM IN A CONKER MATCH, MATE! GOOD TO SEE YOU AGAIN.

JUST THE THREE OF US, SERGEANT — MYSELF, MY ASSISTANT AND ONE SIGNALLER. NOW LEAD US TO THAT HILL YOU PASSED.
VERY GOOD, SIR.

The spotter party moved out —
WE HAVE TO CIRCLE WIDE TO DODGE ANY JERRY LOOKOUTS.
NOT TOO WIDE, SERGEANT. TIME WASTED MEANS MORE FLAK FOR MY BATTERY.

THERE'S THE HILL, SIR. A HEDGE AND A DITCH WILL GIVE US COVER GOING UP.
CARRY ON, SERGEANT.

Later, on the hill —
JERRIES!

THEY MUST BE DIRECTING THE FIRE OF THOSE GUNS, SIR.
USE OF SMALL-ARMS COULD BRING MORE JERRIES ONTO US. THOSE TWO HAVE TO BE DEALT WITH QUIETLY.

ME OLD TRENCH COSH'LL FIX THEM TWO, SIR.
HUM, ER, CARRY ON AGAIN, SERGEANT.

Ted Hicks went into action —
ACH! WAS IST DAS?

URGH!

GOOD WORK, SERGEANT. NOW TO LOCATE THOSE GUNS.
YOU DON'T EVEN NEED FIELD GLASSES FOR THAT, SIR. WE'RE ALMOST ON TOP OF 'EM — TWO JERRY 50-MIL ASSAULT GUNS.

FIRE ORDERS! FREDDIE TROOP RANGING. HE-117, CHARGE THREE — LOAD.

Four ranging rounds came whistling over —
NOT BAD! RIGHT FOUR HUNDRED, ADD TWO HUNDRED — AND WE'VE GOT 'EM!

FIRE FOR EFFECT! THREE ROUNDS GUNFIRE.
HELLO, SUNRAY! FIRE FOR EFFECT!

25-pounder shells pounded the enemy assault guns —
REPORT TARGET DESTROYED. THE WAY IS CLEAR FOR BATTERY COLUMN TO PROCEED.
HELLO, SUNRAY. TARGET DESTROYED!

HEY, SPIKE, WANNA SEE WHAT PUTS THE THUMP IN MY COSH? I'VE CARRIED IT FOR LUCK EVER SINCE MY DAD MADE IT FOR ME FROM A CHUNK OF OLD IRON IN THE FACTORY.
IT LOOKS LIKE LIKE A — WHY, YOU CHEATING CROOK! SO THAT'S HOW YOU BUSTED MY CONKER-THIRTY.

THERE'S NOTHING LOWER THAN A BLOKE WHAT'LL CHEAT AT CONKERS.
STOP FOOLING AROUND, YOU TWO. WE'RE HEADING BACK TO BATTERY!

SPIKE, I JUST DON'T CARRY FIFTY MARBLES ABOUT WITH ME THESE DAYS. HOW ABOUT SETTLING FOR A BAR OF RATION CHOCOLATE?
HOW ABOUT TWO BARS?
THE END

SPORTING Smiles

WHAT A TIME FOR A GAME OF LEAP FROG!
crown paints

AND TO THINK I ACTUALLY ASKED FOR THE BALL!

I'M GETTING THE HANG OF THIS GAME NOW!
15

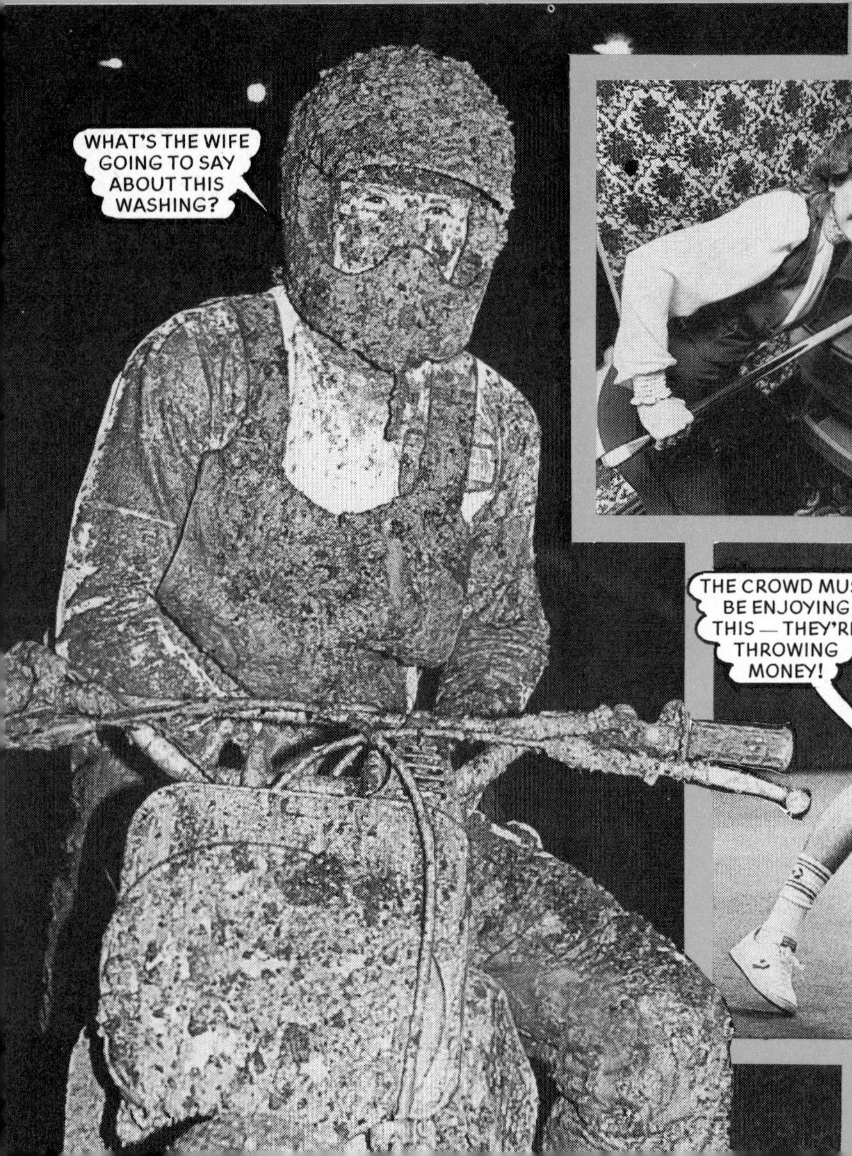

WHAT'S THE WIFE GOING TO SAY ABOUT THIS WASHING?

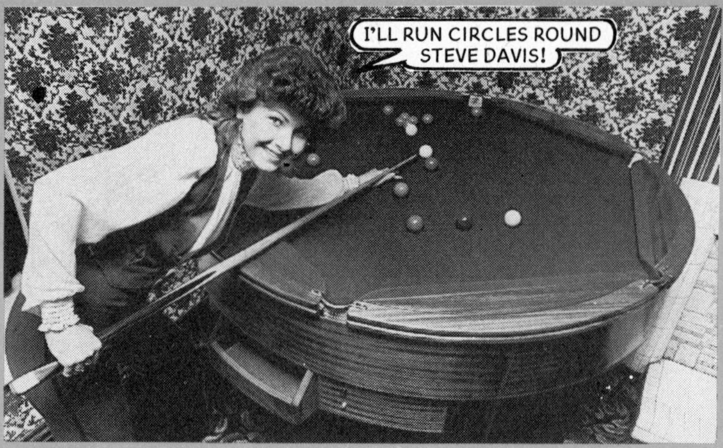

I'LL RUN CIRCLES ROUND STEVE DAVIS!

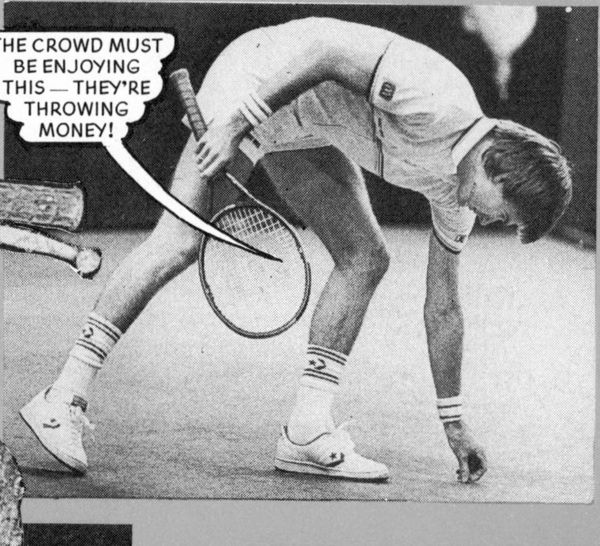

THE CROWD MUST BE ENJOYING THIS — THEY'RE THROWING MONEY!

The Leap of the Long Lances
AIEEEE! SWIFT HEELS SHALL KILL THIS PALEFACE. MY AXE SHALL TASTE HIS . . . ARGHHHH!
THE VARMINTS IN THIS NECK OF THE WOODS SURE DON'T SEEM NONE TOO SOCIABLE!
Canada in 1854 was a place of danger and hardship for men like Jeb Turner, who dared to blaze new trails in the wilderness. Hard weather and wild animals were a constant natural hazard, as were warlike Indians, ever ready to kill the stranger to their land.
THIS ARMY SCOUTING JOB MIGHT NOT BE DULL, BUT IT MAKES A FELLOW WONDER IF HE'LL EVER GET ROUND TO DRAWING A PENSION!
KILL THE DOG WHO SLEW OUR BROTHER!
Jeb made it safely back to the fort.
STILL GOT YOUR SCALP THEN, JEB. THE MAJOR WANTS TO SEE YOU RIGHT AWAY. GOT ANOTHER LITTLE JOB FOR YOU.
SHUCKS! AND ME PLANNING ON A WEEK'S SLEEP AND EATING ME A COUPLA DOZEN MEN'S RATIONS.

KNOW ANYTHING ABOUT BLACK SKULL MOUNTAIN, JEB? BECAUSE THE ARMY HAS ORDERS TO MOVE THERE RIGHT SHORTLY.
HOME OF THE CHOWAGA, KNOWN TO OTHER INDIANS AS THE LONG LANCES. YOU AIM TO TANGLE WITH THEM AND YOU HAVE A RIGHT SCRAP ON YOUR HANDS.

THE CHOWAGA HAVE BEEN HITTING THE TAME PLAINS INDIANS FOR TOO LONG, JEB. TIME THEY WERE BROUGHT TO HEEL.
I'LL TAKE A LOOK-SEE, MAJOR. BY THE TIME YOU GET YOUR FELLOWS TO THE MOUNTAIN, I SHOULD HAVE A GOOD IDEA OF THE LAYOUT FOR YOU.

A few days later —
SO! THE PALEFACES COME FROM THE EAST TO FIGHT RED AXE. TO IMPOSE THEIR WILL UPON THE CHOWAGA.
THEY CAMP AT THE FOOT OF THE MOUNTAIN, BRAVE ONE, BUT THERE IS ONE MAN WHO BRAVES OUR MOUNTAIN TRAILS ALONE AND MOVES DOWN THEM LIKE ANY CHOWAGA!

Jeb was having trouble!
HAVE TO MAKE THIS RIGHT QUICK BEFORE HE GETS CLOSE ENOUGH TO USE THAT PIG STICKER.
YOU WILL DIE EVEN AS MY BROTHER.

HECK! MORE OF THEM AND NO TIME TO RELOAD. I'LL HAVE TO FIGHT LIKE A CORNERED GRIZZLY TO GET OUT OF THIS ONE.
THERE'S MORE THAN ONE WAY TO USE OLD BETSY!
UGHHHHH!

YOU'RE IN TOO MUCH OF A HURRY, FRIEND!

But then —
AIEEEE! THE DOG IS DOWN. LIKE THE STAG BEFORE THE WOLF.

ONE MORE BLOW AND OUR BROTHERS ARE AVENGED.
SO DIE ALL WHO OPPOSE THE MIGHTY CHOWAGA!

NO! THAT ONE FOUGHT WELL ENOUGH FOR HIS CHANCE OF LIFE. RED AXE HAS SPOKEN.
AS EVER IT WILL BE AS YOU SAY, RED AXE!

Later —
YOU SHALL ATTEMPT THE LEAP OF THE LONG LANCES, AS IS THE RIGHT OF ANY WORTHY FOE TAKEN.
I'VE HEARD OF THIS LEAP, AND IT'S NOT ONE MANY HAVE MADE WITH ANY LUCK!

An hour's walk away —
THERE IS YOUR CHANCE FOR LIFE. REACH THE OTHER SIDE AND YOU WILL BE SAFE FROM THE BRAVES OF RED AXE FOR ONE MOON.
BY THUNDER! IT WILL TAKE ONE MIGHTY HOP TO CLEAR THAT GAP!

HERE GOES! AND IF I FALL SHORT, IT'S GOODBYE OLD JEB TURNER!

WILL I MAKE IT?

TOOK MORE OUT OF ME THAN I THOUGHT! I'LL HAVE TO BE QUICK OR MY STRENGTH WILL BE GONE!

THE DOG FELL SHORT. HE HAS USED THE CHANCE THE LEAP OFFERED FOR LIFE AND DESERVES TO DIE.

SWIFT ELK'S LANCE WILL FINISH THIS.

ONE THROW WILL — ARGHHH!

RED AXE GAVE HIS WORD. SWIFT ELK WOULD HAVE BROKEN AND DEFIED THAT WORD!
THAT RED AXE FELLOW SURE SAVED MY NECK THERE!

HE IS A WARRIOR TO RESPECT!
A MAN OF HIS WORD THAT ONE. I'M JUST SORRY HE IS AN ENEMY AND NOT A FRIEND!

A month later, at the foot of Skull Mountain —
AT THE WORD, LADS. UPON ONE KNEE AND A VOLLEY INTO THE HEATHEN!

THE RED-COATED ONES HAVE BLUNTED OUR CHARGE. COURAGE IS AS NOTHING AGAINST THE BALLS AND MUSKETS THE FOE USE SO WELL!

Soon —
THEY HAVE LOST, JEB. RED AXE ALONE MADE IT BACK TO HIS MOUNTAIN AND ONLY BECAUSE SOME BRAVES COVERED HIS FLIGHT.
THIS IS NOW A ONE-MAN JOB, MAJOR, FLUSHING THAT ONE OUT. KINDA LIKE TO BE THE ONE WHO TACKLES IT.

And so —
BY JINGO! RED AXE PLANNED AN AMBUSH AND I NEARLY FELL FOR IT.
THE WHITE ONE IS AS QUICK AS THE WINTER FOX.

SO WE SHALL DECIDE IT WITH THE BLADE. I ALMOST FEEL REGRET I SHALL NOW KILL YOU.
IT IS I WHO SHALL FEEL THAT WHEN MY BLADE IS RED.

YOU MIGHT BE HOT STUFF WITH THAT PIG STICKER, BUT IN KNIFE BUSINESS YOU HAVE A LOT TO LEARN!
UGHHHHH!

A few minutes later —
COME TO, UH? GUESS I CLOUTED YOU HARDER THAN I FIGURED.
AND NOW YOU TAKE RED AXE TO YOUR BROTHERS, TO SHUT HIM IN A CAGE LIKE AN ANIMAL.

I'M NOT TAKING YOU IN. WE ARE GOING FOR A LITTLE WALK TO A PLACE NOT FAR FROM HERE. A WALK I TOOK A LITTLE WHILE BACK.
THE LEAP! THIS ONE IS GIVING ME THE SAME CHANCE THE CHOWAGA GIVES THE FOE HE THINKS IS A WORTHY ONE.

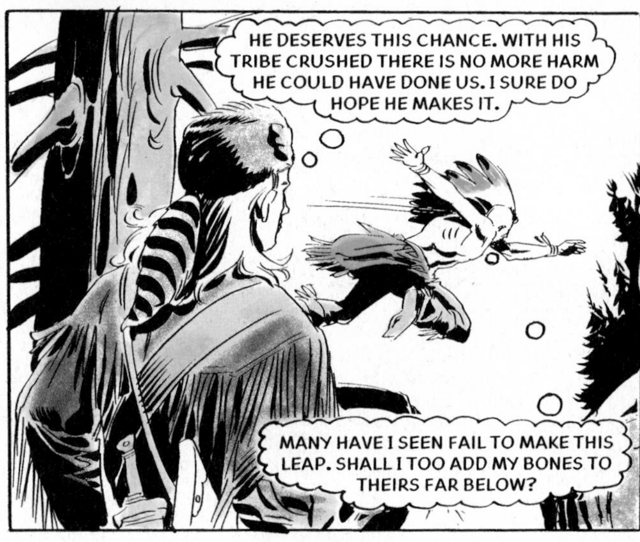
HE DESERVES THIS CHANCE. WITH HIS TRIBE CRUSHED THERE IS NO MORE HARM HE COULD HAVE DONE US. I SURE DO HOPE HE MAKES IT.
MANY HAVE I SEEN FAIL TO MAKE THIS LEAP. SHALL I TOO ADD MY BONES TO THEIRS FAR BELOW?

BY THUNDER! HE MADE IT. AND AIN'T THAT JUST ALL RIGHT BY ME!

I SHALL REMEMBER YOU. MAY THE GREAT SPIRIT GUIDE YOU DOWN SAFE TRAILS.
YOU TOO, RED AXE, MAY YOU TALK AS AN OLD MAN IN YOUR PEACEFUL LODGE OF THE TIME YOU MADE THE LEAP OF THE LONG LANCES.

Later —
SO HE GAVE YOU THE SLIP. AND IF JEB TURNER CAN'T PICK UP HIS TRAIL, NO ONE CAN.
WAAL, MAJOR. YOU COULD SAY IN A WAY THAT WAS ONE REDSKIN WHO WAS ONE JUMP AHEAD OF ME!
THE END

The medieval kings of England were an odd lot, liable to do strange and extravagant things. Here are a few examples!

Henry I could be a pleasant companion at times, but he was a hard man nevertheless. He punished one of his daughters for rebellious conduct by having her dragged through a frozen moat!

Henry II was subject to terrible fits of anger, and during these he would sometimes bite his page's shoulder, or even roll on the floor, gnawing the straw in fury!

In Italy on his way to a crusade, Richard I saw a peasant with a fine hawk and seized it in a rage. But unlike in England, Italian common men were allowed to keep hawks and the man's friends chased Richard away.

In Palestine, Richard I found that Saladin, the Moslem commander, had destroyed Ascalon, and decided to repair the fortifications of the town. He set an example to his soldiers by getting to work himself, and when the Duke of Austria would not do the same, Richard gave him a hefty kick!

King John was a tyrant and oppressed or plotted against everyone who came in contact with him. But he was a great coward, and it is recorded that when he fled in battle, he did so howling!

Edward I made a bet with the royal washerwoman that she would not ride to hounds and come in at the death. The lady accepted the challenge and rode so well that she got to the front and won the bet!

Kings and their families did not always agree. Edward I was so annoyed when his son, later Edward II, asked a favour for a friend that he seized the prince's hair with both hands and pulled it out in clumps!

THE EYES OF IYA

Iya — the ancient god of greed. From exactly where the ruby-eyed idol came was lost in time. But did it have the power to evoke greed in those who saw it? Judge for yourselves!

How it came into the possession of Marcus Centus, a retired Roman general, he would never say — but he was known to have a quick sword for anything he coveted!

MINE! AND IT SEEMS TO REGARD ME WITH SOMETHING LIKE INTELLIGENCE!

Thaxus was a regular visitor. Wealthy vineyard owner though he was, he coveted the idol as soon as he saw it.

MAGNIFICENT! I MUST HAVE IT. NAME YOUR PRICE, CENTUS.
IT'S NOT FOR SALE!

It was the Festival of Light. No servants were present to see greed get the better of Thaxus.

WHAT ARE YOU DOING?
I MUST HAVE THE IDOL — AT ANY COST! IT WAS YOUR MISTAKE TO GO INSIDE THE BEAR'S CAGE TO GOAD IT! EVEN IF IT IS HALF-DRUGGED!

FAREWELL, CENTUS. THOUGH I DOUBT YOU WILL WHEN THE BEAR WAKES FULLY. AND WITH EVERYONE AT THE FESTIVAL NO ONE WILL HEAR YOUR CRIES. THE IDOL SHALL BE MINE!
YOU CAN'T DO THIS! LET ME OUT OF HERE!

It was as he got the idol home that Thaxus saw something strange about it.
THE EYES SEEM TO GLOW! AN UNEARTHLY LIGHT!
YOU SENT FOR ME, MASTER?

Thaxus was a hard master—
WE GO TO THE VINEYARD. WORK HAS TO COME BEFORE ANY FESTIVAL.
YES, MASTER.
YOU FAT SLUG. I'D LIKE TO DROWN YOU IN YOUR OWN WINE.

Then Bara, the servant, saw the idol — and set in it rubies that would make him rich for the rest of his life!
IF I COULD BUT HAVE THOSE STONES! NO MORE GROVELLING TO SUCH AS THAXUS!

At the vineyard—
AFTER WE HAVE FINISHED HERE YOU WILL FEEL MY LASH ON YOUR BACK, YOU IDLE DOG!
I THINK NOT THIS DAY, THAXUS. I HAVE HAD ENOUGH OF YOU AND YOUR CURSED WHIP!

Bara awaited his chance, and when Thaxus was careless enough to stand under a cask of wine swinging from a gantry, the scheming servant released the heavy load!
ARGHHHH! NO!

Bara was free, his master crushed by a barrel of his own wine. A quick visit to Thaxus' villa gave Bara the idol.

I SHALL HIDE THIS IN THE HILLS UNTIL LATER, THEN RETURN TO DISCOVER THE REGRETTABLE ACCIDENT TO MY MASTER.

But a careless step at this height could be fatal—

AIEEEE! I'M GOING TO FALL. SAVE ME!

And it was!

The idol of Iya fell too, down a fissure into a cave — there to lie and wait!

Time passed, and Italy was eventually led into war by Mussolini, a dictator as powerful as any old-time Roman emperor, with arrogant followers—

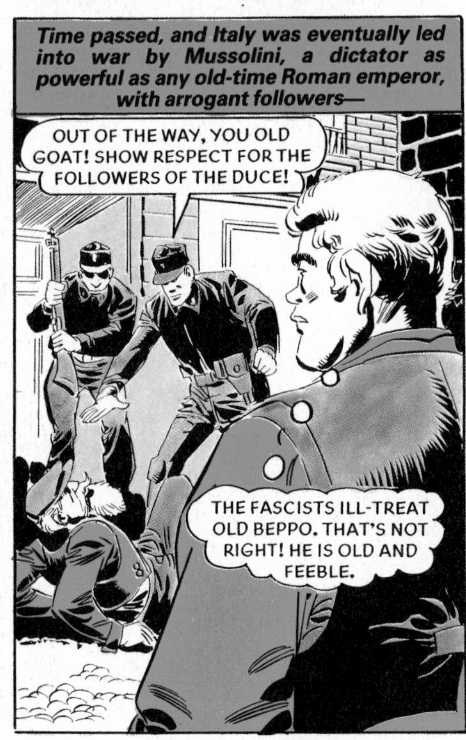

OUT OF THE WAY, YOU OLD GOAT! SHOW RESPECT FOR THE FOLLOWERS OF THE DUCE!
THE FASCISTS ILL-TREAT OLD BEPPO. THAT'S NOT RIGHT! HE IS OLD AND FEEBLE.

BULLIES DESERVE ALL THEY GET. TRY AND GET THAT INTO YOUR HEADS!
CAFF
I THANK YOU, GINO. BUT THE FASCISTS MAKE BAD ENEMIES!

Orders were issued to arrest Gino Valla, but this proved hard to do!

YOU MEAN YOU COULD NOT BRING IN ONE MAN?
BUT WHAT A MAN! WE COULD NOT OVERWHELM HIM, SIR, AND HE ESCAPED OUR RIFLE FIRE.

So it was that Gino fled to the hills and forgot the war, living alone in peace.

A FINE DAY. PITY ITALY SHOULD LET THAT FAT CLOWN, MUSSOLINI, LEAD HER INTO WAR AND SUCH MISERY.

But at last the war came to Gino, in the shape of three British deserters—

WHEN ARE WE GOING TO GET SOME GRUB. I'M STARVING!
ALWAYS WHINING, YOU ARE! MOAN, MOAN, MOAN!

Dan "Shifty" Shills could be relied on for only one thing — to moan!

Bert Oates was an ex-convict. If a thing wasn't screwed down, he'd steal it!

Sam Fogg didn't like the Army, or Italy, or anything else!

Gino greeted the newcomers courteously. Since deserting, the trio had had it rough, and jumped at his offer of a meal—

I WELCOME YOU TO SHARE MY HUMBLE TABLE.
BIG, DUMB OX. BUT IF THERE IS GRUB GOING I'D DINE WITH MUSSO HIMSELF!

I LIVE ALONE. THE WAR DOESN'T INTEREST ME.
IT DOESN'T US EITHER, SINCE WE SHOT THAT SERGEANT AND HOPPED IT!

It was as Gino was showing them a hiding place in case of a German patrol that the evil trio first saw the idol.

THAT LITTLE HORROR'S STONE EYES MUST BE WORTH A FORTUNE!
COR! THEY LOOK LIKE BLINKIN' RUBIES!

But Gino was not going to let anyone remove the idol—
I THINK IT EVIL AND IT WILL DO MUCH HARM IF IT ENTERS THE WORLD!

BETTER IT STAYS HERE. HERE IT CAN DO NO HARM.
HERE IT CAN'T PUT ME ON EASY STREET, YOU BIG APE.

The deserters could not get the idol out of their minds. Only Gino stood between them and its ownership.

Three plans were put into operation by the trio — none telling the others what was afoot!
YOU KEPT OUT OF THE WAR THEN, MATE.
I HELP THE PARTISANS. THEY ARE FIGHTING THE PEOPLE THAT ARE BAD FOR ITALY.

When Gino was off guard, Shills made his sudden move—
OOPS! I SLIPPED!

Back at the hut, Oates was also planning Gino's death—
BIT OF LUCK FINDING THIS MINE IN THE WRECKED TRUCK BACK THERE. THIS SHOULD GO WITH A BANG. NOW I'M GOING FOR THAT IDOL.
Fogg soon found out where Gino was!
WHAT THE —? ARGHHH! I'M FALLING!

Fogg, too, was planning murder—
WHERE IS THE BIG APE? I PINCHED THIS RIFLE OFF HIM SPECIAL!

Shills did not know that at that moment Gino was safe but out cold on the rock ledge — with Fogg at the foot of it out for good!

I'LL JUST GET A TORCH. THEN OFF TO THAT CAVE AND WHAT IS COMING TO ME!

None of the three knew about the cache of explosives in the hut, hidden by Gino for his friends, the partisans.

Shills entered the hut, and stepped squarely onto the mine. That in turn set off the stored explosives.

In the cave, Oates heard the explosion—

WHAT THE HECK? COULD A BLINKIN' MINE MAKE A BANG LIKE THAT?

The concussion of the hut's exploding contents sent rocks thundering down, blocking Oates' exit from the cave forever!

NO! NO! I'M TRAPPED IN HERE.

Gino never could work out what had happened to his three guests, nor why the explosives in the hut should become so unstable.

I'LL HAVE TO BUILD ANOTHER HUT. AT LEAST THAT CAVE IS BLOCKED. THAT EVIL LITTLE IDOL CAN DO NO HARM NOW!

Oates had the idol all to himself.

CAN'T ANYONE HEAR ME? LET ME OUT!

THE END